KOTTAS ON DRESSAGE

KOTTAS ON
DRESSAGE

ARTHUR
KOTTAS-HELDENBERG

with Julie Rowbotham

Kenilworth Press

Text © 2010 Arthur Kottas-Heldenberg and Julie Rowbotham

First published in the UK in 2010
by Kenilworth Press, an imprint of Quiller Publishing Ltd

British Library Cataloguing-in-Publication Data
A catalogue record for this book is available from the British Library

ISBN 978 1 905693 05 4

All photographs by and © Ewald Willibald
(except those on pages 13, 14 and 15 which are from the author's collection)
Artwork by and © Maggie Raynor
Designed and typeset by Paul Saunders

Printed in China

Kenilworth Press

An imprint of Quiller Publishing Ltd
Wykey House, Wykey, Shrewsbury, SY4 1JA
Tel: 01939 261616 Fax: 01939 261606
E-mail: info@quillerbooks.com
Website: www.countrybooksdirect.com

CONTENTS

ACKNOWLEDGEMENTS

I am delighted that my daughter Caroline was willing to be used as the model for the photographs in this book and am most grateful to Ewald Willibald for his time and patience in taking the photographs.

I am also most grateful to the late Jennifer Sewell, founder of Training The Teachers of Tomorrow Trust, and her husband Tom and daughter Alex Cookson for letting me use their home at East Whipley Farm for meetings with my publisher John Beaton and for their constant support.

I appreciate very much the hard work of my co-author Julie Rowbotham and the excellent artwork supplied by Maggie Raynor and the editorial skills of Martin Diggle. Andy Fitzpatrick has very kindly read the proofs and his comments have been most helpful and Claire Lilley assisted with the translation.

CHAPTER ONE

THE KOTTAS PHILOSOPHY

I have been involved with horses all my life. My parents had the oldest riding school in Vienna and I started riding from the age of two and a half on my own pony. Other children would play with their toys; I would ride my pony.

My maternal grandfather ran a haulage company and, as I grew up, my parents expected me to join the family firm. However, much to the surprise of my parents, I decided to try to enter the Spanish Riding School as an Elève (trainee). Having been very successful at riding from a young age, I succeeded in joining the School and started my training in 1960. I became Assistant Rider in 1964, progressing to Rider in 1969. In 1981 I became Chief Rider, and in 1983 Riding Master. I became First Chief Rider in 1995. I left the Spanish Riding School in 2002, and retired in 2006.

My philosophy of training and riding was shaped by the Spanish Riding School. It is the hope and desire of the Spanish Riding School that it sets a good example of upholding the principles and values of classical horsemanship. The Spanish Riding School is living proof that the classical way is the right way. Horses need time in their training. It is amazing to see a horse 25 years of age trained in this way still able to enjoy his work.

The Spanish Riding School has international acclaim. As well as being of great historical interest for Austria, it sets an example that the whole equestrian world should acknowledge.

Arthur Kottas with some young equine pupils.

Here, based on its teachings, are my thoughts on the important aspects of training:

- To stay fit and healthy over a long period of time, the horse must be physically and mentally fulfilled and understood by the rider.

- The rider shapes the horse.

- The key to a good rider is a correct, well-balanced seat: to ensure a light connection between the hand and the horse's mouth, the rider must be balanced.

- The horse must work from active haunches, over a swinging back, to the horse's mouth and back to the rider's hand.

- Most problems are related to the horse's contact with the bridle.

- If the horse is not going well, tomorrow is another day: you can't perform to the maximum every day.

- Take time, but do not waste time.

- If there is something that does not work well, take a step back.

Horses are my life. I always see the horse as a partner. He must be trained slowly and patiently. Every new horse is a new experience.

Favory Alea I in piaffe.
(*Author's collection*)

LEFT
The author training a
young horse.
(*Author's collection*)

RIGHT
Riding in a competition.
(*Author's collection*)

BELOW
Performing a pirouette
at a competition.
(*Author's collection*)

Riding an extended trot. (*Author's collection*)

CHAPTER TWO

THE RIDER'S POSITION

Before any rider can think in terms of training a horse, they need to have a sound, correct position – and every rider needs to pay attention to position throughout their career, to ensure that good practice is maintained and developed.

WHY A GOOD SEAT IS SO IMPORTANT

- The right posture gives you security and comfort; it will influence the stability of the rider/horse combination and determine any change of balance.

- It is the major aid; everything else is only ancillary.

- It is the most important tool of communication between horse and rider: any change of posture is a strong aid to the horse.

A good position must be desired, controlled and mastered. There is no real riding without a good position. For example, it is absolutely physically impossible to collect a horse without having a very good seat, because the rider's back, legs and chest cannot give the aids.

A superficially correct but physically tense seat will create stiffness and anxiety in the horse. Only if the rider is free from such tension can the horse be relaxed. A theoretically correct posture that does not allow the horse to move freely and lightly is only an illusion and a pretence. It sometimes manages to impress the public, but the horse is not convinced!

Only a balanced seat allows the horse to be comfortable, both mentally and physically. A rider in the wrong position, out of balance, or stiff, will prevent the horse from relaxing and keep him from developing and muscling up harmoniously. Every exercise, every stage of training, becomes difficult, if not impossible.

The best seat is the one that allows the horse, in any given exercise, to be in balance and develop impulsion (forward thrust) with minimum interference from the rider.

One factor in establishing a good seat is having a good mental picture of your body. Therefore, take active notice of your body: feel your balance, your positioning; be aware of any stiffness. Only then will you sense your horse and be in harmony with him. Harmony between horse and rider is our goal!

THE ELEMENTS OF A GOOD SEAT

If we wish to improve the way we sit in the saddle it is necessary first to become familiar with the ideal rider position, and then to work to reproduce this ideal in our own riding.

The aim of every rider should be to help rather than hinder the horse; to encourage the free flow of energy and movement through his body and to influence and control that energy. To accomplish this, the various elements of the rider's own body must be aligned correctly – with head, shoulders, hips and heels positioned on an imaginary vertical line drawn through the centre of the body and the centre of the saddle. The rider should almost appear to be standing, rather than sitting on the horse – that is to say, the impression should be that, if the horse were to be taken away, the rider would land with knees slightly bent, but otherwise in a balanced standing position.

The upper body should stretch upwards from the hips to the crown of the head. The head is relatively heavy, so the rider must always try to carry this weight in perfect balance – set straight upon the neck, not tilting to one side; with the eyes looking straight ahead and not down to the ground. The chin should not be allowed to jut forwards, as this would mean that the neck is no longer straight and the head is unbalanced. The shoulders should be held level; back and down, but without tension; if the shoulders are high and tense the

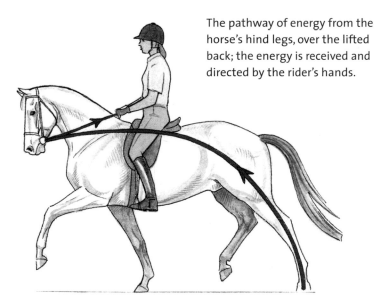

The pathway of energy from the horse's hind legs, over the lifted back; the energy is received and directed by the rider's hands.

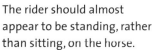

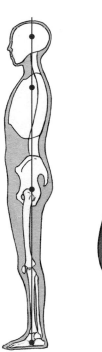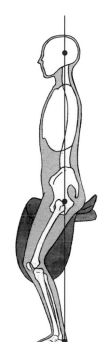

The rider should almost appear to be standing, rather than sitting, on the horse.

rider's lower back will be stiff and unable to move with the horse, and any tension in the upper body will be reflected in the reins.

The arms should hang down softly from the shoulders, with the elbows bent and the hands held just in front of the saddle. The arms, elbows and hands must all be relaxed, and the hands must not be held too high. The reins, hands and forearms should all be on a straight line running from the bit to the rider's elbows. If this line is broken, the direct contact between horse and rider will also be broken. With this in mind, the hands should continue the line of the forearms when seen from above. The thumbs should be uppermost, but the hands should be held with the little fingers slightly closer together than the thumbs.

It is important that the rider has control of the section of the spine which connects ribcage and pelvis, as this is the most mobile section of the backbone. The spine should not be allowed to hollow either forwards or backwards, but should support the ribcage with an 'upward' feeling. There should be no tension in the spine – if the rider's back is stiff, the horse's back will be unable to swing: neither should the spine be floppy, which would result in the rider being unable to use the seat to influence the horse. The rider's back should be able to follow and absorb the movement of the horse's back; a feeling of 'controlled relaxation' in the spine will allow this to happen.

The pelvis should be upright, with weight taken on both seat bones and the pubic bone – this is known as the three-point seat. The rider should sit in the centre of the saddle with equal weight on both seat bones. Correct positioning of the lower spine will help to position the pelvis correctly. If the spine is hollowed forwards the pelvis will automatically tilt forwards, putting extra weight on the pubic bone; if the spine is allowed to sag backwards the pelvis will tilt backwards, which will put more weight on the seat bones.

The lower body – from hips to feet – should stretch down. There should be no tightness or gripping with the knees, thighs or calves; the legs should be 'around' the horse, with the lower legs stretching down to give the aids. It is important that the heels be kept down: this ensures that the calf muscles are flexed and toned. If the heels are raised the calf muscles become soft and the legs cannot be used effectively; the rider will be relying on the spurs (if worn), to give the aids – which will not be applied in the correct place. This mention of strength in the calf muscles does not mean to say that the legs should be clamped on the horse's sides, or necessarily used strongly – but that they should be in a position whereby light, quick, touches are effective. This will not be the case if the muscles are slack.

The horse must learn to respond to the correct leg aids applied on the appropriate area of his body – the leg applied at the girth has a different meaning from the leg applied behind the girth. Of course, this also means that the rider's legs must be controlled and positioned correctly to give the intended aids.

The length of the stirrup leathers should be given attention as this governs the amount of bend in the legs – which, in turn, affects the rider's balance and depth of seat. Adjusting the leathers so that the stirrup iron can be pulled into the rider's armpit while the arm is held out with the fingers touching the stirrup bar usually gives a good, working length. It is an error to ride with the legs too long in the belief that this will improve the seat – on the contrary, the seat will be weakened and the rider will be continually struggling to achieve balance. On the other hand, riding with the leathers too short, and therefore with too much bend in the legs, will also reduce the depth and stability of the seat.

The feet should be held parallel to the horse's sides: if the toes turn out the rider will be using the wrong part of the calf to give the aid. The stirrups should be underneath the balls of the feet.

MY ADVICE ON POSITION

Overall

- Do not look primarily for the 'beautiful posture' on horseback – rather, look for the right posture, at the right time, and you will automatically have a beautiful posture.

- Watch watch how a good rider moves with the horse in slow motion.

- Work on your seat while someone is lungeing you: you won't have to worry about going forward and straight, and you will be able to concentrate on your body.

- Your strength and your balance in the saddle depend on your position, and on your equilibrium; in no way do they depend on the strength of your legs and hands. The seat should be deep with a light leg contact. Your torso, your arms and hands will then be able to relax, be in place and become light.

- Keep your upper torso motionless, your shoulders still and your lower back supple.

- A well-inflated ball bounces on a hard floor: if you tense your legs, if you squeeze with your thighs or your knees, you will bounce up and down in the saddle.

- Only when your hips are loose will you be able to let your upper body relax.

- Relax the lower part of your face, smile from the inside, and you will be able to relax more easily.

- You have to relax each part of your body – your entire body – and especially your lower back, your upper back, your thighs, your legs and your ankles. For this you should point your toes toward the ground (possibly without stirrups) and raise them again, several times.

- Sit tall in the saddle – as though you were a tree. Stretch your legs and toes down like roots reaching for water. Stretch all the way up through your spine – like the tree growing towards the light.

The chest

- Make sure your upper body is upright. Imagine kitchen scales: the front end and the back end of your horse are the two pans of the scale, and your upper body is the beam. Any action of the upper body will influence the balance of the pans.

- If you try to relax your upper body without relaxing your thighs, calves and ankles, you will work hard for years with very little result. Let your lower body be flexible, and you will be surprised by the effect on your upper body.

- Working the back, the aids of the back, the seat and the upper body are essential in dressage: everything else is only ancillary. 'Hold' your horse with your abdomen and upper body and 'give your hands forwards' to the horse. If your upper body and your legs support your horse, all the conditions are in place for giving the hands.

- Always keep your shoulders parallel to the horse's shoulders.

- Look in the direction of the ears of your horse, then you will always stay in tune with him.

- Do not jut your chest forward too much, instead, think of your belly button travelling forward toward the horse's ears and let your shoulders hang down. Whatever your physique is, you will look slimmer and more elegant.

The legs

- The shoulders, the seat bones and the heel of the outside leg should be on the same vertical line. This is easiest to achieve by stretching the legs downwards.

- Do not put your legs in one fixed point – let them loose to free the upper body. If you want a lazy horse and to exhaust yourself, squeeze with your legs. If you want a brilliant horse, active and relaxed, let go with your legs, forget your leg muscles while staying reactive, attentive and relaxed.

- Relax as much as possible, but control your thighs, the backs of your knees, the legs, ankles and feet.

- If your heels are down too much, your lower leg will be unsteady. The tip of the foot rests softly on the stirrup. The ankle has to stay flexible. Being able to put the heel up or down shows the beginning of relaxation.

- Touch the horse with your calf or your spur (ZAP!), for example in trot or in canter.

- Never stay tight with your legs, always act in an intermittent manner (touch, let go, touch…).

- The legs alone really do not make the horse go forward: the key to impulsion (forward thrust) is in the horse's frame of mind. The legs indicate, and stay relaxed. Touch your horse, whether with calf, heel or spur, with an electric touch, lightly and fast. Then immediately take the leg away.

- The spur is only the end of the leg; it has to stay relaxed, with light and short touches. Horses have extremely fast reflexes, much faster than humans. Therefore, act fast and precisely.

- Your legs can reassure the horse and calm him down, *on the condition that they stay relaxed*. Seek to develop legs that reassure, frame and guide the horse.

- Practise, as often as possible, reducing or ceasing the forward aid completely with your legs (the classical French term for this is *descente de jambes* – see also lowering the hands). You will achieve lightness and your horse will be more brilliant.

The hands

- The rider's hand goes all the way to the shoulder.

- For each exercise, seek the best position possible for the hands, in the small space between your belly button and the base of the horse's neck.

- The optimum height for the rider's hands is one fist above the horse's withers (may be lower on a young horse).

- The sensation in the hands must be easy and effortless.

- Keep your hands still as much as possible (with a supple wrist).

- Before using your hands, always use your upper body and a forwards driving leg aid: give your hands back to the horse ('give him his mouth') and hold him with your chest and belt.

- Close your fingers firmly (without pulling) while using the legs, until the horse submits (or yields) by softening to the contact.

- Practise 'giving with the hands' (or softening the contact) as much as possible – in classical French terminology, *descente de main*. The crux of this is not so much the physical repositioning as the *reduction in pressure of the hand* and, consequently, the rein.

- When the horse is correctly balanced, cease all action of the hand (and leg) that has been employed to achieve this balance.

- The 'softening or lightening' of the hands (or reduction/cessation of the leg aids) is done every time a desired result is obtained. In some circumstances, it may be expedient to cease both leg and hand effects (*descente de main et des jambes*) to check whether the horse retains his balance and rhythm under these circumstances.

- The horse must not, of his own volition, change anything in the exercise.

- The hands remain quiet and passive whilst the horse maintains his attitude, forward thrust, his gait and the exercise. The hands will ask again only if there is a risk of change in the horse or if the rider wants to modify the exercise.

- Always take before you give, and give only when the horse submits.

- The wrists should be slightly flexed inwards.

COMMON FAULTS IN POSITION

As we should now have a clear, mental picture of the ideal rider position, let us consider what can go wrong. Positional faults can escalate like a rolling snowball – what starts out as a minor deviation from the correct position in one area of the rider's body can go on to affect every other part, with unfavourable consequences to the horse's comfort and way of going. To emphasize the point, any deviation from the correct alignment mentioned earlier – the head, shoulders, hips and heels positioned on a straight line running vertically from the centre of the saddle – is a fault which should be recognized and corrected.

Faults in the longitudinal plane

These are faults in which, essentially, the rider's weight is wrongly positioned and thus influences the horse incorrectly in terms of being too far 'back' or 'forward'.

Sitting behind the vertical

Here, the rider sits with the upper body leaning backwards and, to counter-balance this, the legs move forwards. The pelvis will be tilted backwards, with the rider's weight carried mainly on the seat bones. In the same way that a person carrying a backpack with straps which are too long has two options for comfort – either to round or to hollow the back – so will the horse who has to carry a rider seated like this will either hollow his back or over-round it in an attempt to carry the weight comfortably. The reins may well be too long, or the rider's arms and hands may be extended and lifted out of their correct position. In either case the rider will lose effective contact with the horse's mouth. The effectiveness of the rider's legs will also be reduced, as the leg aids will not be given in the right place on the horse's sides

Collapsed upper body and rounded shoulders

This fault is often seen in riders who sit at a desk all day. A rider with this postural problem will never be able to use the seat correctly to influence the horse, as the back must be upright to give the aids either to slow the horse down or to send him forward. The human head is heavy, and to ride with the head and shoulders so far in front of the vertical can only encourage the horse to go on the forehand. The freedom of the arms will be restricted, making the rider more likely to be insensitive and heavy with the hands.

Pelvis tilted forward and back hollow

Here, the rider's weight is taken on the pubic bone, which effectively dis-courages the horse moving forwards. The rider's back will be stiff and unable to swing – a state of affairs that will be mirrored in the horse's back. The

Rider's postural faults
in the longitudinal
plane.

Behind the vertical   Collapsed upper body   Pelvis tilted forward and
                             and rounded shoulder   back hollow

stability and sensitivity of the rein contact will be lost because of tension and
unsteadiness in the arms. This posture is sometimes caused by the attempts of
a relatively inexperienced person to ride with the stirrup leathers too long;
the rider's back is then hollowed in an attempt to anchor the insecure seat in
the saddle.

All these postural faults involve a deviation from the ideal vertical alignment
of the rider's head, ribcage, pelvis and heels. This misalignment reduces the
rider's ability to absorb the thrust of the horse's movement and results in
tension and loss of balance.

Lateral misalignment

Further problems arise if the rider's lateral or horizontal alignment is not
correct – in other words, if the shoulders and hips are not level, or if the head
is held to one side. The horse is very sensitive to weight, and will move underneath an unbalanced rider in an attempt to balance the weight and carry it
more comfortably. This will result in the horse not being straight – the hooves
of the hind legs will not move on the same track as the hooves of the forefeet.

  The fundamental cause of much lateral misalignment is the collapsed hip.
Many riders collapse the inside hip on a turn or circle. This is a good example
of the 'snowballing' effect of bad posture. It begins with the rider allowing the
ribcage to collapse over the inside hip; this moves the seat over to the outside

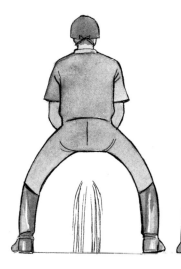
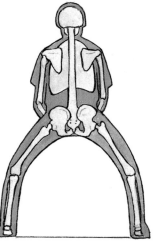

Lateral misalignment of the rider. Upper picture shows correct posture; lower picture shows the elements of crookedness.

Correct, straight rider position

- The rider allows the ribcage to collapse over the right hip.
- The seat moves over to the left side of the saddle.
- The left leg hangs down lower than the right.
- The right knee and toe lift and rotate outward.
- The right shoulder is lower than the left.
- The left elbow lifts up and away from the body.
- The head is tilted to the right.

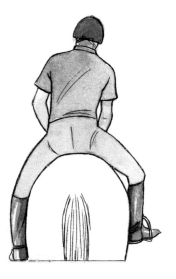
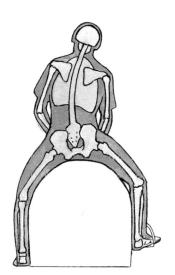

Crooked rider position

of the saddle, which means that the outside leg will hang lower than the inside leg. The inside knee will lift and rotate outwards, as will the inside toe. The inside shoulder will drop lower than the outside shoulder, which will lift the outside elbow up and away from the body. To complete the picture, the head will be tilted to the inside.

As a result of all this confusion the horse will be unable to execute correctly the movement he is being asked to perform, and no matter how many times he is asked to repeat it he will not improve until the root cause – the rider's position – is put right.

FREQUENTLY ENCOUNTERED PROBLEMS IN POSITION

Do the legs have to be tight on a horse?

NO! – to be a strong rider does not depend on the power of the legs, but on the general balance of the rider and on the weight/counterweight formed by the legs hanging down, relaxed and touching the horse softly, but never tight.

To tighten the legs or to use the legs vigorously, tires, discourages or exhausts the rider: it does not result in forward thrust but tenses, turns off and bores the horse. Correctly timed and well thought out actions, fast and relaxed, where the legs touch the horse with care and are immediately retracted are efficient, economical and discreet.

'More legs' is an idea to banish from riding!

My trainer says my hands are too hard

A hard hand is a one that has no feel, is incapable of giving, asks with strength, at the wrong time, with no subtlety. It is damaging to the physical and moral well-being of the horse!

If I discount the fear, the lack of experience or the mental brutality of the rider that sometimes produces hard hands, most of the times it comes from the absence of relaxation, the lack of balance and a generally bad seat. It is then an overall problem. To deal with this issue, try to determine whether your seat is in balance.

Your legs could be tight, and/or 'stuck' to the horse – such legs will prevent you from sitting softly. If you are bouncing, your back is stiff, and your hands are inevitably hard. Do not forget that your hands start at your shoulders on horseback! Relax your legs and buttocks, sit deep in the saddle and your back will be soft…your hands will become better.

If your general posture is good and your legs are relaxed, be careful to let your arms fall down naturally, hands low, with the arm/forearm angle rather open. Round your wrists slightly towards the inside, keep your fingers softly closed.

Aid with your hands in an intermittent manner, and cease to aid as soon as the horse answers. If he does not react, do not harden your action: cease the aid and repeat it immediately.

Finally, it is essential to be relaxed on your horse. 'Good hands' result from an harmonious rider (developed by a correct seat and empathy for the horse). The rider needs to know when to resist and when to give at the moment the horse submits; they have to be in soft contact with the horse's mouth.

Work toward these goals…

THE IMPORTANCE OF POSITION – A SUMMARY

When you see a rider whose position and balance are correct the picture will be one of complete harmony; it looks as if the whole business of riding is easy and effortless, and this is how it should be. As we progress with our training we will be asking the horse to obey commands which become ever-more complex, refined and precise. For instance, we will be asking him to differentiate between a passive leg aid applied behind the girth to prevent his quarters moving out, an active leg aid applied at the girth to encourage him to engage his hind leg – and yet another aid asking him to move his hindquarters away from the rider's leg. We will be using the seat both to collect the horse and to ask him to extend his stride; to ask for both a half-halt and a full halt. Our weight will be on the left seat bone to ask for both leg-yield to the right and half-pass to the left. If we riders do not have absolute control over every part of our body, how can we hope to be able to communicate our wishes to the horse?

Before attempting to teach a horse to respond to these precise aids, the rider must be physically capable of giving them. The horse whose rider has unsteady hands, an unbalanced seat and a varying leg position will be unable to differentiate between the conflicting signals he is being given at every stride. For this reason an inexperienced rider should be taught on an experienced horse, and an inexperienced horse should be taught by an experienced rider.

The key to successful riding lies in the balance and stability of the seat. It should be the ongoing aim of every rider, no matter how experienced, to correct and perfect their seat – and the best way of doing this is to be taught on the lunge, which we will consider in the next chapter.

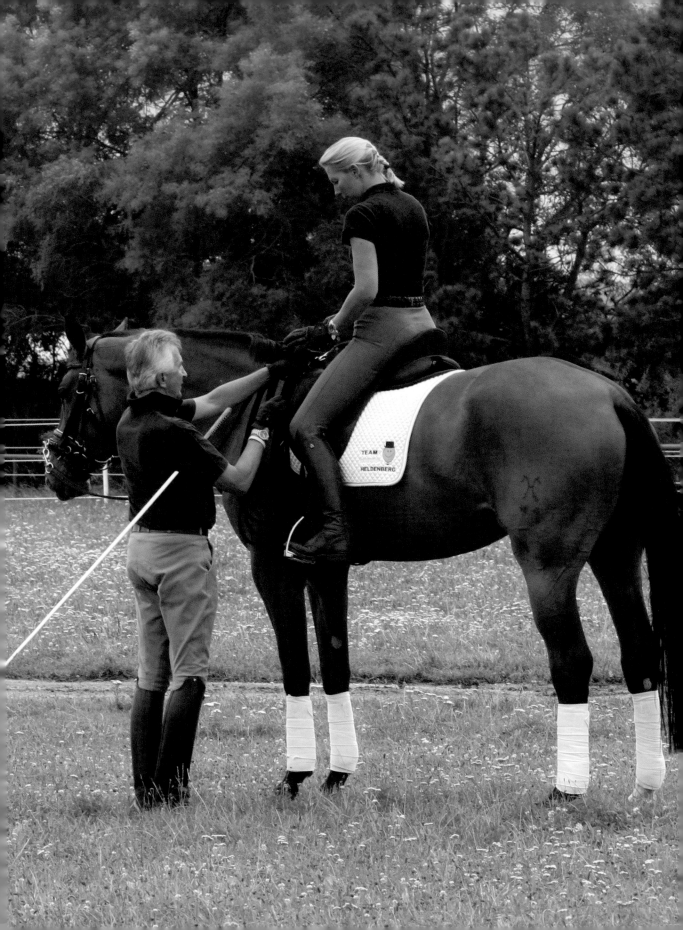

CHAPTER THREE

TRAINING THE RIDER ON THE LUNGE

In the previous chapter, I discussed the basic elements of correct posture. In this chapter, I would like to explain the role that work on the lunge can have in developing good posture of the rider at all gaits, and to outline some relevant exercises.

At the Spanish Riding School, novice riders spend a minimum of two years on the lunge before they progress to riding the horse unassisted in the arena. Students are lunged by other riders and the instructor stands outside the circle, from which position he can more easily see if the rider's weight is central or whether it has slipped to the outside; if the rider's shoulders are parallel to the horse's shoulders, or if the rider's outside leg has moved from the correct position.

Many of the problems experienced by novice riders arise from lack of balance – the rider cannot follow the horse's movement with seat and body and so has to 'hold on' with either the reins or the legs. The rider must learn to keep the correct body alignment – both vertically (head, shoulders, hip and heel) and horizontally (equal weight on both seat bones; shoulders and head level) at all times.

The rider's back must swing with the swing of the horse's back, but if there is any stiffness in the lower spine and the hip joints this will not be easy. As well as correcting position, the instructor can ask the rider to perform a series of exercises specifically designed to improve balance and suppleness, and to help the development of a deep seat independent of the reins.

The horse used for such exercises on the lunge should be quiet and well-trained: a young horse who cannot keep a steady rhythm, or a horse with a stiff back, will not assist the rider to relax and find the correct balance; a poorly schooled horse will not offer the correct responses. The horse should be fitted with side reins; the bridle reins should be knotted to allow the rider's arms to be free. The horse should be lunged on a large circle. The lunge rein should be attached to the middle ring of the lunge cavesson, which must fit the horse properly.

Before beginning training sessions on the lunge, it can be helpful if a novice rider has an understanding of how the horse moves at each gait; how this will affect the rider's position and how the body must respond in order to be in harmony with the horse. Although these matters are discussed further in the individual chapters on the gaits, they are summarized here.

THE WALK

The walk is a four-time movement. The sequence of steps at the walk is left hind, left fore, right hind, right fore. At least two feet are in contact with the ground at all times; there is no period of suspension. This makes the walk a relatively easy gait to sit, but although the rider is not thrown upwards at every stride there is still plenty of movement – both from side to side and up and down – which must be absorbed by the rider's seat and upper body.

As the left hind lifts, the left side of the horse's back will sink. Once the left hind touches the ground underneath the body, the left side of the back will lift up when the hind leg pushes the horse's weight forwards. This sequence is repeated as the right hind leaves the ground and moves underneath the horse, but now it is the right half of the back which drops and then lifts. The rider's pelvis should follow these movements of the horse's back, while the upper body remains still. The rider should have the feeling of growing upwards from the waist whilst relaxing downwards from the hips.

As the left hind lifts and the left side of the back dips down, the horse's ribcage swings to the right; as the right hind lifts, the ribcage moves over to the left. These movements will be felt against the rider's legs, and the rider should learn to recognize them, for this swinging of the ribcage combined with the rising and falling of the horse's back indicate which hind leg is lifting and which is actually underneath the horse's body at any given point in the stride. This

The horse's head moves slightly to the right as the right fore lands

As the right hind lifts, the right side of the back dips down, and the ribcage moves over to the left.

Recognizing movements of the horse's body at walk.

knowledge will allow a crooked halt to be felt and corrected, and will enable the aids for walk/trot and walk/canter transitions to be timed to perfection.

The horse's head and neck also move with each stride. The head moves slightly sideways towards the advancing foreleg, and also drops down a little as the horse's weight is taken on to that leg. The rider must be careful to follow these movements with the hand, and not to restrict the head and neck through tension in any part of the arm. This does not mean that the hands must move backwards and forwards with every stride – giving and taking with the fingers should be sufficient to keep the contact without restricting the head.

Lunge exercises at walk

Throughout these exercises it is important that the rider's weight is taken equally on both seat bones, and that the pelvis remains upright in the correct position.

The stirrups should be crossed over the saddle – riding without stirrups is an excellent way to develop a deep and balanced seat.

- Rotating the head slowly in a circle, right and then left.

- Circling one arm backwards, then forwards. Repeating with the other arm, then with both arms together.

- Circling both shoulders backwards.

- Holding the arms out at the shoulders, then turning from side to side from the waist.

- Lifting one leg away from the horse while 'growing upwards' with the upper body, then closing the leg back again. Repeating with the other leg.

- Lifting one leg away from the horse and swinging the leg backwards and forwards from the hip. Repeating with the other leg.

These exercises can also be used to warm up before beginning a schooling session; with a trustworthy horse they can done off the lunge, or they can be performed just as effectively on a stationary horse. (We tend to forget that the rider, as well as the horse, needs to be warmed up and prepared for exercise – this is especially true of a rider with a sedentary occupation. Also, this work can be very taxing for a rider, and it is better to stop before the rider becomes tired and tense.)

HERE AND OVERLEAF These exercises can be performed either as part of a lungeing session or, as shown, to warm up the rider on a stationary horse before work begins.

Warm up exercises continue overleaf ▶

THE TROT

Trot is a two-time gait; two beats are heard as the legs move in diagonal pairs – left hind and right fore followed by the right hind and left fore – with a period of suspension between the two. The rider's seat has to absorb the upward thrust which occurs each time the horse springs from one diagonal to the other. There are two ways of achieving this – to ride the trot either rising or sitting.

Rising trot

When rising to the trot the rider rises out of the saddle as one diagonal pair of legs are in contact with the ground and sits down again when the other diagonal touches down. Most novice riders master this rhythm very quickly, but to maximize comfort and effectiveness of the aids, there are various adjustments which should be made to the rider's position.

The fault most often seen in novice riders is that of rising too high out of the saddle. In this case, the rider actively instigates the upward motion, throwing the body upwards from the knees. The correct method is to allow the horse's momentum to push the pelvis out of the saddle, but rather than lifting the ribcage up, the hips should move forwards towards the hands. In this way the rider will not be gripping with the legs, or tense in the calves and knees, but will be relaxing through the legs – allowing the legs to be 'wrapped around' the horse. Instead of landing heavily, the seat will touch down softly into the saddle; because the upper body is not moving up and down the hands will be still and steady.

The basic principles of correct position detailed in the previous chapter still apply to rising trot. In summary:

- Straight line from ear, shoulder, hip and heel.

- Eyes looking straight ahead, head up, chin slightly back.

- Shoulders back and down without being tense.

- Upper arms relaxed, with the elbows held softly by the side.

- Straight line running from the elbow through the rein to the bit.

- Weight taken equally on both seat bones and on both stirrups.

- Heels down and toes pointing towards the front.

Sitting trot

Both novice and not-so-novice riders frequently experience problems when trying to sit correctly to the trot. Sitting trot makes great demands on the rider's seat and back, as considerable suppleness is required in the section of the spine which links ribcage to pelvis. The pelvis should move with the horse's back, enabling the seat to be continually in contact with the saddle. The rider must be able to absorb the two-time motion of the horse's strides by giving softly with the pelvis and spine – yet without losing the feeling that the spine is supporting the upper body. If the spine is allowed to be too slack the rider's upper body will wobble – the head will nod, and the arms and hands will move up and down along with the ribcage. If the spine and pelvis are too tense, the rider's seat will leave the saddle at every stride, putting the rider out of balance to the point of having either to grip with the legs or hang on with the reins to retrieve it. At sitting trot the rider's balance is everything – and this balance is not easy to achieve.

The mechanics of sitting softly to the trot are, of course, directly linked to the horse's movement. As we have seen, the horse moves at trot by pushing and lifting his body from one diagonal pair of legs to another. As his feet touch the ground, his body will drop; at this point the small of the rider's back 'swings' very slightly, moving the hips a little forward. This allows the impact to be cushioned and absorbed by the buttocks and pelvis. As the horse begins to lift up in the period of suspension, the small of the rider's back should flatten; this straightens the pelvis and allows upward momentum to be absorbed by the seat and thighs. These back and pelvic movements should not be exaggerated; the rider should be doing no more (or less!) than following every movement of the horse's back. When working on the lunge at trot the rider should seek to retain a mental image of perfection and try to emulate it.

Lunge exercises at trot

Rising trot

For these exercises the rider should use the stirrups, but they should also be ridden without!

- Dropping both arms by the sides and relax for a while, then lifting the hands to the correct rein-holding position without actually holding the reins in the hands. (The reins can be knotted and laid on the horse's neck.) Repeat several times.

- With hands in the correct position, taking time to perfect the feeling of rising correctly – that the seat is not lifting too far out of the saddle, but rather that the hips are moving a little way forward towards the hands. When rising, weight of rider's upper body should be allowed to 'drop to the knees'. This can be done with one, or both, hands on the saddle until the rider is in balance with the horse.

- Practising slowing down the rhythm of rising: the horse's rhythm should slow down accordingly.

- Practising walk/trot/walk transitions by slowing down the rising trot (as above) then sitting to trot and asking for a transition to walk by sitting a little more heavily and allowing less movement in the lower back. Then asking the horse to trot on again.

- Going from rising to sitting trot, and back to rising again.

Sitting trot

To be performed with or without stirrups – this can be extremely tiring for the rider, so frequent breaks will be required:

- Letting both arms hang down at the sides, behind the legs.

- Holding one arm at riding level and the other behind the back. Changing arms (without holding the reins).

- Holding on to the front of the saddle with one hand, circling backwards and forwards with the other arm. Changing arms.

- Circling both arms backwards and forwards.

- Holding both arms above the head.

- Putting both hands on the hips.

- With elbows bent, putting the fingers on the shoulders.

- Holding both arms sideways from the shoulders and turning the upper body from side to side.

- Transitions from trot /walk /trot using the seat and back (as described in section on rising trot).

- Rising trot without stirrups – this is a good way to learn how to close the knees.

- Rider should take time to feel the movement of the horse's back beneath the saddle; tries to find the correct way of finding their balance (holding on to the front of the saddle with one hand may help). The rider should practise relaxing and allowing the pelvis to move with the horse while keeping the upper body upright and firm.

Throughout these exercises the upper body and pelvis must remain in the correct position, with equal weight on both seat bones. The lower legs should not move away from their correct place on the horse's side (the inside leg on the girth and the outside leg just a little further back). The rider's shoulders should remain parallel to the horse's shoulders.

THE CANTER

Each canter stride of three beats is followed by a moment of suspension. The outside hind begins the sequence, followed by the inside hind and outside foreleg together and then the inside ('leading') – fore. The horse then has all four legs off the ground while the outside hind is moving forward to begin the next stride. The horse makes an up-and-down, forward-to-back rocking motion as he repeats this sequence, and the danger here is that the rider is tempted to rock the upper body along with the movement – tipping forward as the horse's head lifts and backwards as the head drops down. This technique may give impressive results on a toy rocking-horse, but will seriously hinder and unbalance a real one!

The correct way to sit to the canter is for the rider's body to remain upright throughout the whole sequence – allowing the lower back to swing a little as the horse's body moves downwards and to flatten as the horse moves up in the period of suspension. The seat should always be in contact with the saddle and the legs should not move from their position on the horse's sides – but the lower arms and hands should be soft enough to follow the movement of the head and neck, keeping a steady contact with the mouth.

Lunge exercises at canter

To be performed with stirrups at first; without stirrups when the confidence and balance of the rider allow:

- Holding on to the front of the saddle with one hand, circling the other arm forwards and backwards. Changing hands.

- Rotating both arms backwards.

- Placing both hands on the hips.

- Lifting both arms above the head.

- Transitions canter/trot/canter using the back, seat and legs, with the hands held in riding position without the reins. The aids should be given by the person lungeing the horse.

- Rider should take time to concentrate on the movement of the horse beneath the seat; feeling the three beats of the legs and the moment of suspension; feeling the horse's body rising and falling; holding upper body still and upright while pelvis follows the movement of the horse.

HALF-HALT

The half-halt should also be taught on the lunge. The rider should practise leg/seat/hand co-ordination, learning to ride the half-halt correctly by using even back, seat and leg pressure, and lastly closing the fingers. This asks the horse to slow down a little and engage his hind leg further underneath the body – the rider then immediately allows the horse to move forward by re-leasing the pressure of the fingers. This requires considerable co-ordination on the rider's part (and, to reiterate the point made earlier) an unschooled horse will not respond to a correctly given half-halt. The rider on a well-schooled horse on the lunge does not have to worry about controlling direction and thus can concentrate on applying the aids and will understand how a correctly performed half-halt should feel when the horse gives the correct response.

GENERAL POINTS

These exercises on the lunge can be very strenuous for the rider, particularly if riding without stirrups – and a tired rider will not benefit from any further work. It is best to stop at frequent intervals to allow the rider to stretch and relax any part of the body which is tense and painful – the toes can be rotated to relieve stiffness there; the arms stretched, and the head rotated to soften the neck. This should be done with the horse walking on a long or loose rein; he too will need to stretch and relax. It goes without saying – but is especially relevant at canter – that throughout the lungeing session there should be frequent changes of rein.

Lungeing the novice rider is an excellent way of ensuring that the principle of using seat, leg and rein – in that order – has been understood and can be applied. Making transitions without using the reins ensures that the rider does not rely on the hands to bring the horse down through the gaits. The rider must learn to effect downward transitions by applying a steady leg, resisting slightly with the lower back, sitting deeply into the horse – and, last of all, closing the fingers of the hand.

Towards the end of the lungeing session it can be revealing to take away the side reins and stirrups and ask the rider to try to work the horse in a rounded outline. A rider who cannot achieve this needs more instruction on the lunge before attempting to ride the horse free in the arena.

WORKING THE ADVANCED HORSE AND RIDER ON THE LUNGE

Lungeing is sometimes considered to be primarily a technique for training novice horses and riders, but in fact it remains of great value for advanced individuals and horse/rider combinations.

When working the advanced horse and rider on the lunge, the trainer is not only able to assess and help the rider's position, but can also help with the whip if the horse is lazy in transitions, or to add impulsion to the more difficult movements, such as piaffe.

The horse is ridden in the normal way; the rider has both reins and stirrups, but side reins are not fitted. The rider must use seat and legs to keep the horse moving forward on to the bit. The trainer should observe the rider's

OPPOSITE
Lungeing remains of great value for advanced individuals and horse/rider combinations.

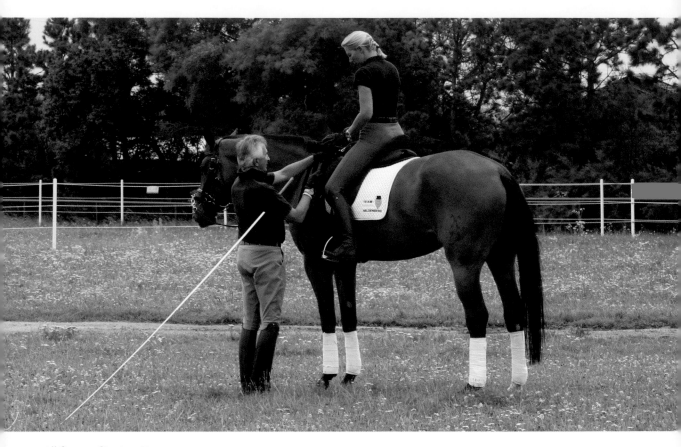

All forms of instruction require close communication between trainer and rider.

position, making sure that the legs, seat and hands are used correctly and that the rider's shoulders are always parallel to those of the horse.

The horse begins to work in collected walk. He is then asked for shoulder-in and haunches-in. It is important that the rider keeps the horse bent correctly and this entails correct positioning and use of the outside leg behind the girth to control the quarters. The horse is then asked to work in collected trot, and once again to perform shoulder-in and haunches in. Collection should be maintained throughout all transitions – the horse being encouraged to take more of his weight back on the hind legs rather than just becoming shorter in the neck. Half-pirouettes in walk come next; the hind legs keeping the correct walk sequence on the track while the forehand turns around on the inside of the track. The horse should be very collected, and the half-circle of the pirouette should be very small. The same sequence of exercises should then be performed on the other rein.

Trot/walk/halt transitions should be made, always checking that the halt is square. Then ask for transitions from collected trot to collected canter and returning to collected trot; then from collected trot to counter-canter with flying change back on to the inside lead. This exercise should be repeated on the other rein.

The horse can then be asked to stretch and relax by the rider opening the hands in collected trot – the horse must remain in trot but the neck should move forwards and down. The horse can then walk on a loose rein. The rider can also use this opportunity to stretch and relax.

The rider should then take back the reins and practise collected trot/piaffe/collected trot transitions; here the trainer can help to keep the horse moving forwards by touching him gently on the legs with the whip. Then piaffe/collected trot/collected walk transitions followed by a half-pirouette at walk, and a repeat of the same exercise on the other rein. The lesson should finish by allowing both horse and rider to stretch and relax once more before the rider dismounts, runs up the stirrups, loosens the girth and rewards the horse.

Lungeing in this way should help both horse and rider to improve. Help from the ground will enable the horse to understand what is being asked of him, and the rider will be encouraged to develop an active seat to ride the horse forward and to use seat, leg and rein to collect the horse. He can also learn how to put more weight into the inside stirrup in the correct way.

With advanced horses and riders, it is possible to practise movements such piaffe on the lunge.

CHAPTER FOUR

TRAINING THE HORSE ON THE GROUND

The most important attributes to have when working with horses are gentleness, thoughtfulness and sensitivity. We must ensure from the very beginning, particularly when working with a young horse, that he has a trusting approach to the training and that he enjoys working with us and is not treated as a machine.

A horse needs to slowly get used to everything we need to do with him and not become afraid of – or shy away from – us when we go through the various procedures. The horse must learn and understand that what we do is only for his welfare and to protect him from harm.

When working with horses, we must take our time with everything in order that we carry out our task correctly. To do this is so important in the preparation, education, training and riding of the horse. For steady progress, every moment we spend with our horse has to be utilized constructively right from the beginning.

My personal motto is: we should take time, but not waste it. To reiterate, everything we do has to be done so that the horse understands what we want. This builds trust between horse and rider. We want the horse to be our partner so that he looks forward to his work and enjoys it.

INTRODUCING EQUIPMENT FOR LUNGEING

Correct fitting of basic tack

First, we must attend to the horse's comfort by ensuring that all equipment is properly fitted and adjusted. We begin by putting on the horse's boots or bandages and we do that with the forelegs first and then progress to the hind legs. In the case of a horse who has never previously worn boots on his hind legs, we can make the process of fitting easier by lifting up a forefoot – this makes it safer to attach the boot to the hind legs.

The boots or bandages are not designed to support the legs overly, as this would reduce their strength. Instead, they should protect the legs and tendons from being struck by the shoes and thus prevent or avoid any injuries that might result from this.

Next, we put on both the saddle and bridle. The saddle is taken to its correct position from the front; it must more or less 'slide' back into its correct position.

We should not move the saddle forwards from the back. The simplest and easiest way to find a saddle's ideal position on a horse's back is to use one's hand: the front edge of the saddle's knee roll should sit a hand's width behind the shoulder-blade.

The numnah or saddle pad has always to be straightened and neatly tucked into the arch under the pommel in order not to cause any unnecessary discomfort or pressure on the horse's withers.

It is important to take particular care when attaching the girth that it does not bang against the forelegs as doing so may startle the horse and cause him to jump away, which can lead to accidents and injury.

Since, initially, we only intend to lunge the horse after he is saddled, a lungeing roller is attached over the saddle. Since the straps of the girth should not be fastened too firmly at first, using a lungeing roller has the advantage that the horse can be lunged without causing the saddle to slip. This may be especially beneficial later on. For example, if the side reins are attached directly to the saddle, it may happen that the horse stretches his neck and moves his head forward in an attempt to make himself feel freer. Then, if the girth straps are not fastened tightly enough, this would cause the saddle to slide too far forward. This could cause discomfort, or even a girth gall.

Another important advantage of a lungeing roller is that the horse can be lunged with or without a saddle.

The lungeing roller I prefer has various positions for attaching and adjusting side reins. The top-most rings are attached in the place where the rider's hands would usually be positioned and are used to keep the horse in a higher posture. The middle rings are on a level corresponding to the horse's normal head-carriage and the bottom ones can be used if it is necessary to work the horse in a longer outline. I will discuss various options, in conjunction with the fitting of side reins, in more detail.

For the time being, the next step is fitting the bridle. This is done by, first, lifting the reins gently over the horse's head and neck and then, just as as gently, drawing them backwards into position.

What has to be taken into account whilst doing this is that the horse needs to remain controllable at all times in case he moves away or retreats. Even if he tries to step away one should be able to easily prevent him from doing so.

Then a hand is moved towards the horse's lips in order to prompt him to open his mouth on his own account, as this makes inserting the snaffle a lot easier. Fitting the snaffle correctly is of special importance and one must proceed gently and with utmost care and precision. If the snaffle is to rest comfortably in the horse's mouth, the corners of the lips must not be pulled back too strongly. Also, it is important that the snaffle is not too narrow in width, so that it does not restrict the horse's jaw and lip movements. Another point to which particular attention should be paid when fitting the bridle is that the noseband is not fastened too tightly or too low. The throatlatch, underneath the bridle, should also not be fastened too tightly: one should be able to comfortably place a hand between the fastened throatlatch and the horse's head. This is correct.

It is important to remember that an ill-fitted bridle can lead to the horse's mouth becoming cramped and sore, causing severe discomfort and/or pain. This, in turn, makes a horse restless and lacking in concentration and is more often than not the reason for the horse to resist or go against the rider's aids. Instead of this, a horse should feel comfortable wearing both bridle and bit since this will make it easier for him to learn over time not only to accept the rider's aids but to listen to them and understand them, rather than acting against them.

Tacking-up should never be rushed and must always be done correctly and thoroughly as this is essential for the horse's well-being and thus imperative for the harmony between horse and rider.

Notes on the cavesson

Finally, we fit the cavesson. I consider a cavesson to be imperative when lungeing a horse. Too often, however, the lunge rein is simply clipped on to the snaffle ring. Yet, when lungeing a young horses this is absolutely unacceptable and incorrect!

One must imagine a young horse who has not yet got used to the rein aids and therefore does not understand how to accept or react to them. Suddenly he experiences pulling directly at the snaffle, which, as we know, is attached to the most sensitive part of the horse's mouth!

The most natural and instant reaction of a horse can be, therefore, to resist.

Horses are flight animals, which means that a horse will run away, or at least attempt to do so, when alarmed. In this instance, if a horse is startled and tries to follow his instincts by running away, when we start pulling on the snaffle, we produce a feeling of panic as well as pain. As a natural reaction the horse will now attempt even more strongly to evade this situation. What may then happen is that the horse pulls up his tongue in order to escape the pain or, worse, he actually manages to pull his tongue over the snaffle. All these eventualities can be prevented by utilizing a cavesson.

(The one instance in which it is permissible to attach a lunge rein to the snaffle is when lungeing a horse more advanced in his training on two reins – see later this chapter.)

A good pattern of cavesson has three rings attached at the front – the lunge rein should be clipped to the middle ring. The outer rings can be used for the side reins. They also serve the purpose of enabling us to work a horse who cannot have a bit in his mouth because of a mouth injury or some problem with his teeth.

The cavesson is fitted on top of the bridle. Its cheekpieces are fastened a little more tightly than those of the bridle to prevent it from slipping over the horse's eyes during the lunge work. The cavesson must be carefully adjusted in all respects to prevent potential danger of injury to the horse if he makes any abrupt or sudden movements of his head.

An alternative to the usual practice of fitting a cavesson over a bridle is a specially designed cavesson that enables a horse to be lunged without having to put on a bridle beforehand, because the snaffle can easily be clipped on and off the cavesson. This represents an easier option if a horse is just being lunged and not ridden afterwards (this applies to horses of all ages, not just young

Cavesson and snaffle
bridle correctly fitted
for lungeing.

ones). There is another advantage, as well. With a bridle, the noseband must
be positioned approximately a hand's breadth above the nostrils to allow un-
hindered breathing. Exactly the same rule applies to the cavesson. Therefore,
whenever both a bridle and a cavesson are used one is obliged to make a
compromise: the cavesson is affixed either above or below the bridle's noseband. If the cavesson is fastened too low, it presses on the horse's nostrils and
thus impairs the breathing. If the cavesson is fastened too high, it affects the
application of half-halts to the horse's nose. The use of a cavesson with a clip-
on attachment for the snaffle avoids having to make this compromise and
allows optimal positioning.

FIRST LESSONS ON THE LUNGE

To teach a young horse to work on the lunge the trainer needs knowledge
and experience. The trainer must know how and when to apply the half-halts
with the lunge rein, how and when to use the whip and how much activity to
ask for. (Once the trainer is working alone, the lunge whip should be long
enough to enable the trainer, working on a 20 m circle, to touch the horse
on the shoulder or the quarters with the lash. If the whip is not long enough
to do this, the trainer can walk on a small circle with the horse rather than
stand still in the centre. The size of the lunge circle should be adapted to suit
the horse's level of training, not the length of the whip.) It is fundamentally

important to be aware if the horse is not working correctly, i.e. not working from the hindquarters to the bit, or if the horse is bending just in the neck rather than through his whole body. The confidence to cope with any problems which may arise is also essential. Therefore, a person who is a novice at lungeing should gain experience, under instruction, working with established horses, before attempting to train young horses on the lunge.

Initial education of the horse

In the same way that it would be useless to give a book to a child who has not been taught to read, the young horse cannot be expected to know automatically what is required of him in the lungeing arena. The horse must learn, and the trainer not forget, that every aspect of the procedure must be explained and understood. For the first few sessions it is helpful to have an assistant – one person to hold the lunge rein and the other to handle the whip; this makes the process of educating the horse so much simpler.

The horse is brought into the arena wearing his tack, but without side reins attached to the bit at this stage, the side reins are clipped to the roller out of the way. The lunge line is attached to the central ring of the cavesson. The whip handler will lead the horse out on to the track, whilst the lunge rein handler stands in the centre of the circle. Ideally, a circular lungeing arena should be available – not too small, with a diameter of 20 m or so. If this is not possible, create a lungeing area in a school or on another sound, flat, safe surface by using straw or hay bales. Never lunge a young horse on too small a circle, as this could damage his tendons and ligaments.

The whip handler must walk alongside the horse on the track, to show the horse that he is expected to work on the circle. The horse must gradually be accustomed to accepting half-halts – small checks made with the lunge rein – which ask him to slow down, and also the stronger check which gives the signal to halt. Voice commands should be used in conjunction with the lunge rein signals – 'steady' with the half-halt, and 'whoa', 'stand' or 'halt' with the full halt. The voice should also be used to reward the horse when he has understood or obeyed.

The use of the whip should also be *explained* to the horse – that is, it should not be brandished at him in a meaningless or threatening way. A touch

Arthur Kottas with a horse ready for lungeing.

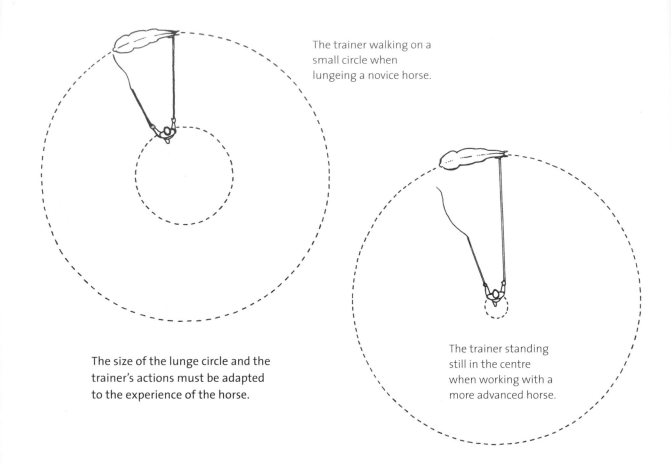

The trainer walking on a small circle when lungeing a novice horse.

The size of the lunge circle and the trainer's actions must be adapted to the experience of the horse.

The trainer standing still in the centre when working with a more advanced horse.

on the shoulder means that the horse should move out on to the circle, while a touch on the hindquarters indicates that he should increase his speed. The horse should be encouraged to move forward and stretch down, and to keep a soft, elastic contact with the lunge rein and also the side reins when used. If the lunge rein becomes loose because of the horse's inactivity, the horse should be sent forwards on the lunge circle with the whip, making sure the hindquarters follow in the direction of the shoulders. If the horse is pulling against the rein this should be corrected by the use of half-halts.

The combination of aids from lunge rein, whip, voice and assistant should be used in a consistent manner to gradually increase the horse's understanding. When asking the horse to trot, the voice should be used in conjunction with a soft touch of the whip on the quarters. If the horse rushes off, or begins to canter (we do not require canter at this stage) a half-halt with the lunge rein should indicate that he needs to slow down and concentrate. When asking for an upward transition the voice should be used with a sharp, upward inflec-

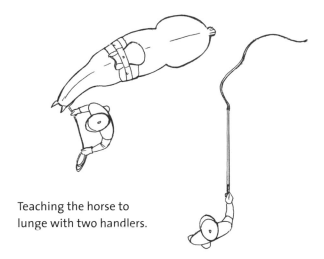

Teaching the horse to
lunge with two handlers.

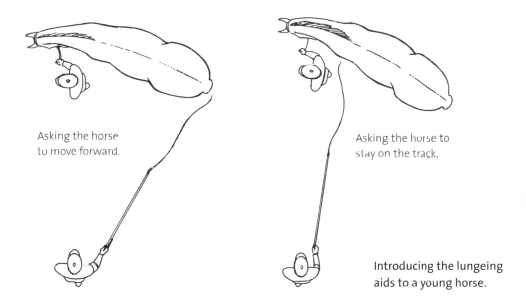

Asking the horse
to move forward.

Asking the horse to
stay on the track.

Introducing the lungeing
aids to a young horse.

tion; when a downward transition is required the command should be long, slow and with downward inflection. For example, to obtain a transition from trot to walk use a half-halt with the rein combined with the vocal command 'and… walk.' These same voice aids will be used when the horse is first ridden: training should be a step-by-step progression for the horse – one thing leading logically on to another. The horse should always understand and be happy with what he is being asked to do before moving on to the next stage in his education. In this way, the trainer will gain the horse's trust and respect.

Another point to remember is that the horse will become less attentive if he is tired, stiff or bored. Therefore, keep the initial lessons short (try to end them *before* this point is reached) and, of course, be sure to change the rein regularly.

As it becomes evident that the horse is starting to understand what is required of him, the whip handler moves away from the horse to stand in the centre alongside the lunge rein handler. (If the horse begins to follow, the whip should be used in the direction of the shoulder to explain that he has to stay out on the track.) The trainer can then start to lunge the horse alone, controlling both the rein and the whip.

To instigate this, the trainer can catch the horse's attention by swinging the arm holding the whip in a circular motion so the horse takes notice of it. (Remember that the aim is to gain the horse's attention and this should

The trainer should constantly monitor the young horse's attention and confidence. The horse in the upper picture is tense and resisting; the horse in the lower picture is relaxed and attentive.

not mean brandishing the whip in a threatening way.) The trainer must watch the horse to ensure that he is working correctly. At this stage in his training the horse should be working with activity (but not speed!), in a steady rhythm with a free shoulder and the neck stretching *forward and down*. The hindquarters should step under the horse's centre of gravity. The trainer must be ready to correct any shortcomings by immediate use of half-halts or the whip.

Introducing side reins

The next stage is to begin work with the side reins attached. These should be adjusted so that they come into play only when the horse reaches for the bit as a result of forward momentum from the active hind legs. The inside rein is adjusted two or three holes shorter than the outside rein to allow for the flexion and bend in the horse's body to the inside: this adjustment must be attended to whenever a change of rein is made. I prefer to use running side reins which fasten on the top rings of the roller, pass through the rings of the snaffle and run back to fasten on either the second or third rings of the roller – depending on the level of head-carriage required – rather than fixed side reins which run simply from bit to roller. The horse should never be pulled down into an outline, but should be encouraged to find the outline for himself through the activity of the hind legs: running side reins are preferable to fixed side reins as they allow the horse the flexibility to do this.

The horse must be taught to keep the contact with the side reins; the trainer should send him forward if he drops behind the contact, and combine half-halts with forward encouragement if he resists by lifting his head. Working correctly – with energy from the hind legs passing over the back to the bit – builds the right muscles in the right places.

Always remember that the purpose of lungeing is to encourage and improve the engagement of the hindquarters, the activity of the back and to get the horse overall to work more closely towards the contact. Therefore particular attention must be paid when lungeing a horse with the assistance of side reins that they are attached correctly *every time*, both in terms of being the appropriate length, as well as the correct height. The most important factor in every kind of training is its correct execution, as only this ensures that a horse develops the right musculature required for a perfect posture, and a correct top line. Because of this, side reins must *never* be positioned too low, as this can cause the horse to go on the forehand and to develop the wrong

Adjusting the side reins in a way appropriate to the horse's level of training is crucial. (Top left) side reins too long; (top right) side reins too short; (bottom left) suitable length for an advanced horse; (bottom right) suitable length for a novice horse.

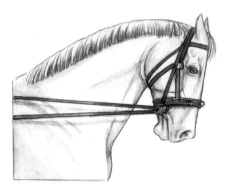

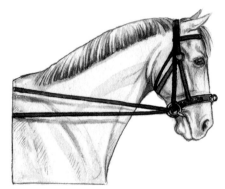

The importance of the horse working correctly on the lunge must never be underestimated.

Horse working correctly from the hind leg over the back to the rein. The spine is lifted, the hind leg engaged, and the face is slightly in front of the vertical.

Horse hollow and lacking activity. The hind leg is trailing, the back hollow and the neck compressed at the poll and base. The nose is behind the vertical.

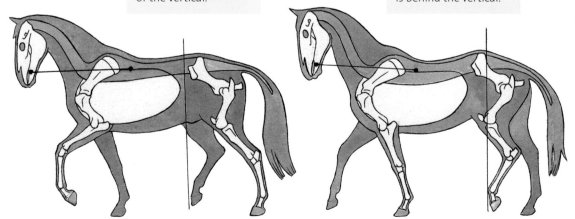

muscles. On the other hand they must *never* be positioned too high, as this can cause the horse to go without the correct use of his back.

The correct attachment of side reins is thus a very delicate matter and it requires a great deal of feeling and experience to be able to adjust them exactly to the required height or in depth; even more so to find the correct length of neck that is necessary. The incorrect application and use of side reins is mainly caused by lack of judgement and/or experience and must be avoided under all circumstances as it does far more harm than good. Training and exercising the horse correctly, however, serves the purpose of improving a horse's outline and expression.

These pictures show the reactions of the whole horse to incorrect and correct adjustments of the side reins. (Top left) A horse resisting side reins that are too short for his level of training; (top right) a young horse not working forward despite wearing side reins adjusted quite long; (bottom left) an advanced horse happily working into the contact of shortened side reins; (bottom right) a young horse taking the contact of side reins suitable for his level of training.

ABOVE, RIGHT AND
OPPOSITE PAGE
Correct work on the
lunge should lead to
active, balanced
movement in walk, trot
and canter.

The next stage

With the horse now understanding what is required of him, and accepting the concept of working forward into correctly adjusted side reins, the accent is on progressive improvement of the gaits and the horse's musculature and overall way of going.

When canter is introduced on the lunge, trot to canter transitions can sometimes give problems for the young horse. Ideally, the horse should not run into canter, but make the transition cleanly without speeding up the trot. If the canter is too fast the horse will be bent to the outside. This can be controlled by encouraging him to take more inside bend by using a half-halt combined with the whip on the shoulder. (With an older, stronger horse, the inside rein can be shortened to try to overcome this problem.) Note, however, that generally speaking the horse's body should be bent evenly on the circle from head to tail; if the neck is excessively bent to one side he will not be able to use his back correctly.

In the downward transition to trot, the voice and half-halts should be used (voice first) to effect the transition.

The repetition of transitions – particularly walk/trot/walk – is beneficial because this sets the horse back on to his hindquarters and so encourages activity of the hind legs.

The trainer should at all times watch closely to ensure that the horse is relaxed (with energy from the quarters passing over the back to the bit); that the movement looks supple and loose with no tension or resistance. The rhythm should be steady but the gaits should develop more cadence as the frame becomes a little rounder and more engaged. The trainer must be ready to spot and correct problems before they become established faults. Remember to reward the horse immediately with a pat or the voice when he has done well.

LUNGEING OVER CAVALLETTI AND SMALL JUMPS

Being lunged over cavalletti is a valuable part of the horse's preparation for ridden work because it is particularly effective at loosening the back and building the back muscles. The horse must look down to see the obstacles and then lift his feet to clear them; by doing this he is both putting himself in the correct shape and increasing the flexion and strength of the limbs – especially the hind legs and the back.

The horse should wear a snaffle bridle and cavesson, but no side reins. Instead, he should be encouraged to lengthen his neck and be fitted with a 'bungie' (a stretchy rubber band) that runs over the poll, through the snaffle rings and between the legs to the roller. This doesn't pull the head down, but encourages the horse to find the way down for himself.

To begin with, up to three cavalletti should be arranged on the circle; these can be tackled either at walk (where the spacing between the poles is narrow – about 0.9 m) or at trot (where the spacing is wider – about 1.4 m). Later on, adjusting the spacing between the poles for trot work will give you more scope for increasing or decreasing the stride. The horse should be calm before attempting the cavalletti, so lunge him first with frequent walk/trot/canter/trot/walk transitions to dissipate some of his energy (but not to exhaust him). He should then be led at walk over the cavalletti, to explain to him that he is not expected to jump over them. When he is happy to walk on his own you may progress to trot.

Lungeing over cavalletti or raised poles helps to loosen and round the horse's back.

Lungeing over poles on a circle helps the trainer to adjust the horse's length of stride.

Be mindful that, when lungeing over cavalletti, the trainer must move on a circle with the horse and not stand still at the centre. You can adjust the length of the horse's stride by altering his position on the circle – the narrow spacing will shorten the stride and the wider spacing at the outer edge of the poles will encourage him to lengthen. Two or three more cavalletti can be added when the horse is working confidently. Change the rein at frequent intervals and don't work the horse for too long – this work can be tiring and the horse should be relaxed at the end of the session.

Towards the end of the training session remove the bungie to see how the horse moves without it – his rhythm and speed should not change, and he should keep his rounded outline.

The next step is to add a small jump (with an appropriately built wing pole on the inside) after three cavalletti, to be negotiated at trot. The horse should stretch down and relax because he is using his back correctly, not because he is being pulled into shape.

You can now progress to lungeing the horse in canter over two small jumps arranged on the circle; an assistant is useful in this exercise to change the wing pole with every change of rein.

Lungeing over cavalletti and jumps not only develops the horse physically, it also provides variety and interest in his training programme.

When lungeing over jumps, it is important to add a pole to ensure that the lunge rein does not get caught on the wing.

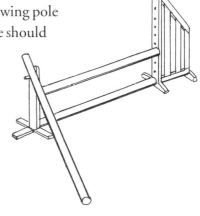

LUNGEING WITH TWO LUNGE REINS

For this exercise the horse does not need to wear a cavesson as the two lunge reins are attached directly to the rings of the snaffle, one on each side. The inner rein runs from the roller, through the inside bit ring, and then to the trainer's hand. The outside rein runs from the bit ring to an outside ring on the roller, then goes around the horse's hindquarters (sitting underneath the tail, just above the hocks) to the trainer's hand. The trainer holds one rein in each hand, with the whip held in its usual position. Side reins are lightly fitted, the inside rein up to three holes shorter than the outside to allow for the bend in the body. When using this method of lungeing the trainer has control of the horse's quarters, which is not the case with the single lunge rein. The outside lunge rein acts to prevent the quarters swinging out; the hind leg moves in the same direction as the forehand, giving the horse more bend. Even on a small circle the horse will move on one track, not falling out with the hindquarters. This will make the horse supple and help him to work on the bit.

The trainer is also able to influence the horse through the bit, which cannot be done with the single lunge rein attached to the cavesson. The whip is used in the normal way to send the horse forward, and the trainer uses the reins to half-halt and to make transitions. This helps to familiarize the horse with the rein aids which will be used when he is ridden – another logical progression in our step-by-step approach. Voice aids should also be used.

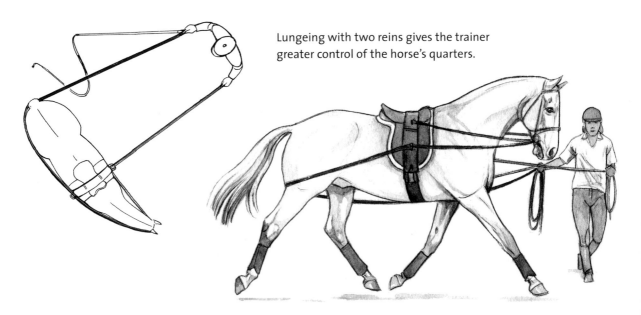

Lungeing with two reins gives the trainer
greater control of the horse's quarters.

Transitions can be performed softly and accurately; the halt can be corrected by asking the hind legs to step squarely using the outside lunge rein. Trot/halt/trot transitions can be practised, as can walk to canter – and even halt to canter when the horse is stronger. Using the double lunge rein helps the horse to work with more and more collection, but this must not be hurried – the muscles need time to develop and strengthen. Working on a smaller circle will help the horse to collect and bend; bringing the shoulder to the inside, whilst making sure that the quarters are not falling out, will encourage the horse to take his weight back. If more bend is needed, keep the outside rein contact and half-halt with the inside rein. When slowing down and stopping, use the same aids as when riding – ask more on the outside rein and push with the whip while keeping a soft contact with the inside rein. The horse must learn to wait for the commands, so the halt must be held until the signal to move on is given.

Remember to change the rein, adjust the side reins and reward the horse. At the end of the training session the side reins can be removed and the horse worked with only the two lunge reins – which should prove that the horse doesn't need side reins to work on the bit.

Through this lungeing programme the horse is taught obedience, discipline and control. He is round and supple; working through his back and on the bit. He is soft, light and active, which will be our continued goal under saddle… and all this achieved with the minimum of stress.

WORKING THE HORSE IN-HAND

As with lungeing in its various forms, working the horse in-hand can make a valuable contribution to his education. This work is a traditional part of classical equitation as carried out at the Spanish Riding School and other classical establishments.

First steps with the young (or novice) horse

To begin work in-hand, the horse should be wearing a snaffle bridle, a lungeing cavesson and a saddle. A lungeing roller to which the side reins are attached should be fitted on top of the saddle – if the side reins are attached to the girth of the saddle there is a risk of the saddle being moved out of place should the horse suddenly pull downwards. There is also the possibility that the straps of the cavesson could be pulled over the eye during half-halts, so it is important that the cavesson is fitted correctly. The horse should wear boots/bandages on the forelegs but not on the hind legs, as it will be necessary to touch the hind legs with the whip. The tail is put up and bandaged, again to enable the whip to be used on the quarters if necessary.

A horse prepared for work in-hand.

The lungeing roller is fitted with various rings – set high, middle and low – to which side reins are attached. (Before fitting side reins you must ensure that the horse is already familiar with their use; if not he could pull backwards, or refuse to move at all, through fear.) As with lungeing, I like to use running side reins which attach to the highest ring of the lungeing roller, run through the bit ring and then attach to the lowest ring. This arrangement has the advantage of allowing the horse to find his own head-carriage rather than fixing the head – as is the case with the more traditional version of side reins. The side reins should not be too short; for a young horse the nose needs to be positioned a little in front of the vertical. The side reins should not pull the horse's head down, rather they should bring the horse into a good outline with a nicely shaped neck. If the side reins are set too low the horse will pull on his shoulders, which will limit his freedom of movement. The whip for in-hand work must be long enough to touch the horse's legs from the trainer's position at the horse's side. When using the whip, the whole arm should be relaxed, but only the hand and wrist should be used to swing the whip.

We work the horse in-hand to introduce and improve collection – a process which will ultimately work towards piaffe and passage. The horse can learn to collect more easily without the weight of a rider on his back, and the trainer can explain the principles of passage and piaffe more easily from the ground than from the saddle. All horses, regardless of age or level of training can benefit from correct work in-hand – it is just a case of adapting the method to the horse's ability.

Before starting work in-hand the horse must be taught to understand the half-halt given from the cavesson. This can be done alone or with two people. If there are two people, the assistant stands at the horse's head holding the lungeing rein, and the trainer holds the whip and stands at the horse's quarters. We begin by asking the horse to walk forward, the trainer encouraging him to do so by using the whip gently at hock level. The handler, standing just in front of the horse's shoulder, vibrates the lunge rein to ask the horse to halt. These half-halts should be soft – as with riding, a heavy and strong rein aid will result in a heavy and strong response from the horse.

This is the first step. The horse begins to understand that he must move forward in a nice round shape, then halt and wait quietly, keeping his rounded outline. Walking on and stopping with a soft half-halt should be practised repeatedly until you are confident that the horse has understood and is happy and relaxed with the procedure.

To familiarize the horse with the whip used for in-hand work he can be stroked gently on the neck and quarters until he accepts the touch of the whip quite happily. The whip will be used either to send the horse forward or to ask him to lift his legs.

We can then continue by asking him to pick up a leg by touching the hind legs right and left alternately, just below the hock, and rewarding him each time he responds. When he has understood and is happy to lift the leg at halt we can ask him to walk on and, by touching each leg as he moves, encourage him to lift the leg a little more and bring it underneath his body. This will result in a more active and collected walk.

A halt that is not square can be corrected by asking the trailing hind leg to move by a tap from the whip.

Working with two people and two lunge reins

The next stage is to work the horse with two lunge reins. The additional lunge rein is attached to the outside ring of the cavesson or the bit ring, runs over the neck at the withers and is held by the trainer. The assistant holds the lunge rein attached to the centre ring of the cavesson and walks, as usual, at the horse's head. The trainer walks to the side of the horse, just behind the quarters, carrying the whip – which is used as mentioned earlier.

Working the horse in-hand; two people and two reins.

Half-halts are given by the trainer with the lunge rein which runs over the withers, but the assistant is there to help support the half-halts if necessary. Trainer and assistant must work closely together during this procedure, and eventually all three participants should unite as one team.

The horse should once again be asked to walk on and halt squarely, with the trainer using both the whip and the lunge rein.

When the horse has fully understood the half-halt and is happy to lift a leg when touched by the whip, he is ready to learn how to collect. He is asked to walk on, and the trainer taps the legs to ask him to move them more quickly. The horse should begin to lift the legs, engage them under his body and eventually pick up a few steps of diagonal movement. When this happens, stop and reward him – and then repeat.

Trainer and horse alone

Once this work is established, you can begin to work with the horse alone, using only the lunge rein attached to front of the cavesson. Walk alongside the horse, in front of his shoulder; you should be able to control his whole body, so don't stand too close or too far away. You must be able to see the horse from head to toe in order to monitor how he is moving. You may either walk backwards, or

Working the horse in-hand; one person and one rein.

sideways, while working the horse, taking big walk steps rather than running. Good co-ordination is required between the hand holding the lunge rein and the hand holding the whip – in-hand work is very skilful, and needs much practice and observation!

Repeat the exercises the horse has already been taught – the half-halt by vibrating the lunge rein, walk to halt, and asking for one or two diagonal steps with the whip. It is important that the horse continues to enjoy his work, so you must always ask yourself if he has understood what he has been taught, and reward him whenever he is good. Make sure you do not forget to change the rein frequently!

As with lungeing, the whip can be used on different parts of the horse's body to correct various problems which may arise. For instance, if the horse begins to move in from the track, the whip can be directed at the shoulder; you may need to touch him on the flanks to ask for more impulsion; or a touch on the croup if the horse is working too high in the croup. If the horse goes haunches-in, you can take him away from the track and straighten him by using the whip on the side of his quarters. This is, in effect, a partial turn on the forehand. It will teach him not to move against the whip, and it is also a good exercise to get the horse to stretch and cross one leg underneath his body, as he will need to do when he begins lateral work.

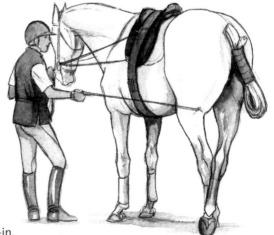

In-hand correction of haunches-in.

By working correctly
with two people and
two reins, the horse can
be brought to a stage
at which he can begin
piaffe in-hand.

Beginning piaffe in-hand

The work we have been doing with our novice horse will, if practised consistently and correctly, develop into the beginnings of piaffe. Correctly performed, piaffe is a diagonal movement, the horse springing from one diagonal pair of legs to the other – but with little or no forward movement. The hind legs should lift one hoof length up from the ground, but the forelegs can lift as high as the horse is able to move them. The feet are allowed to move a maximum of one hoof's length forward at each step. The horse's croup should be lowered, and the poll should be the highest point of the neck. The basis of piaffe is collection. It is quite possible for a horse to be performing a parody of the movement – moving diagonally and with his head held in the correct position – but with the hind legs not engaged underneath his body. In this case the piaffe is incorrect, as the horse is not collected. Collection does not mean only that the horse's frame is shortened, but rather that the horse is able to take a good proportion of his weight back on the haunches. Of course, the horse's back must still be lifted and swinging, allowing energy to be transmitted from the hind legs to the bit. Teaching the horse to collect is a difficult and time-consuming process – but this can be made easier by in-hand work, where the horse is working without the extra weight of a rider.

In-hand work on piaffe should usually be done towards the beginning of a training session, when the horse is fresh. Only with nervous, excitable horses should it be done later in a session, when they have begun to settle.

The work now involved will be a continuation of the training process already begun – helping the horse to collect by taking more of his weight back on the haunches. Because the horse now understands what is being asked of him, we can press confidently ahead with his education.

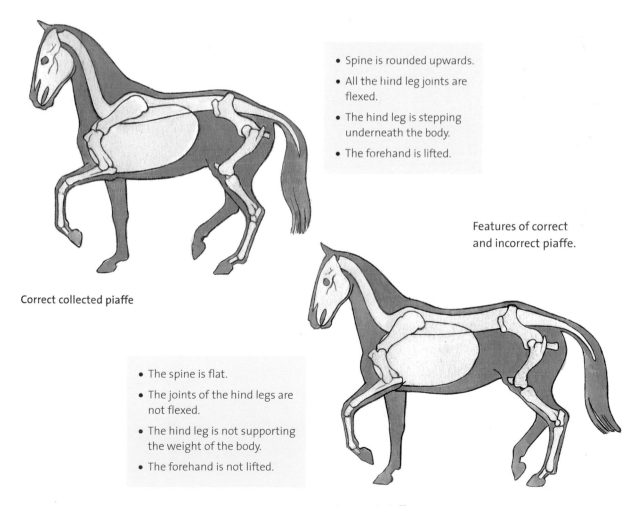

- Spine is rounded upwards.
- All the hind leg joints are flexed.
- The hind leg is stepping underneath the body.
- The forehand is lifted.

Features of correct and incorrect piaffe.

Correct collected piaffe

- The spine is flat.
- The joints of the hind legs are not flexed.
- The hind leg is not supporting the weight of the body.
- The forehand is not lifted.

Incorrect piaffe

CHAPTER FIVE

THE WALK

Fundamentally, to train a horse is to develop the purity of the gaits. Only after he walks, trots and canters with harmony, relaxation and rhythm, in a correct posture, light and vibrant, can the horse start on the harder exercises.

Horses not trained in this progression might still learn complicated and spectacular movements if their rider is skilled, but they will never give the impression of ease, beauty and harmony that shows the signs of good riding.

The true *haute école* (French for 'high school') resides in the perfection of the gaits, starting with the walk.

In the walk, the horse learns to accept the rein, leg and weight aids, as well as how to remain in balance when carrying the rider.

THE WALK IS THE TRAINING GAIT

The slow and soft quality of the walk favours communication between rider and horse. For this reason, it is the most useful gait for helping improve the rider's seat. At walk, problems with posture, balance, muscle relaxation and in some cases even fear, are easier to handle, for both horse and rider.

In the walk, the horse accepts lots of things in his body and his mind in a relaxed manner; he stiffens a lot less, and the exercises are easier. It is important to maintain rhythm, fluency and the length of stride, and the flexibility of the horse's back. Without this it is impossible to proceed with the other gaits.

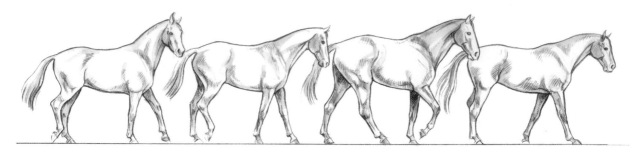

The sequence of
footfall at walk.

What to look for in a good walk

- Suppleness (looseness) through the whole body.

- Abolute straightness

- Maintaining outline

- Rhythm and regularity

- Good collection

L'Hotte's famous maxim: 'Calm, active, forward and straight' sums up the essential qualities of the walk (and it applies to all gaits).

A good walk is defined by how regularly the feet hit the ground: the steps are nicely equal, all of the same length and rhythm. The horse is straight, and he should remain in front of the vertical with his nose. The horse must not be over collected, but he should carry some weight on his haunches. The shoulders are free, the movements of the limbs are free from stiffness. Each hind leg thrusts forwards equally.

The walk should be trained as with the other gaits. It can be improved with walk-halt, halt-walk transitions. Walk on a contact can be schooled by including frequent transitions from collected walk, to medium walk, to extended walk, and back to collected walk. The rhythm should remain constant – it should not become slower or faster.

The horse should stretch forwards and downwards through the body. The reins should not slip through the rider's hands abruptly, but be offered to the horse by opening the fingers.

The horse should not be walked for too long in collected walk as this can affect the over-track of the hind feet in medium and extended walk.

For a horse, straightness encompasses both a mental and physical attitude: it is a state of mind. A straight horse is:

- Straight in the shoulders and the haunches (aligned so that the hind feet follow the fore feet).

- Stretched out by the forward thrust, the 'impulsion'.

- Ready for any change in direction or gait.

Regularity, energy, range and fluidity are constant concerns for the rider. The development of these qualities, day after day, will take the young horse toward the collected walk, which is the principal goal of the work in a walk, and a major goal in the overall training.

How to improve the walk of a young horse

If broken correctly, the young horse goes forward freely in medium walk, in a horizontal balance, the neck relatively low, in a natural position – not behind the vertical. He goes faster in response to any movement of the rider, worries easily, sometimes gets 'stuck', often deviates from a straight line and stiffens in the corners.

The young horse's back still lacks strength when carrying the weight of the rider. It is necessary to muscle up this link between front and hind end until the supple back unites the two ends of the horse. In order to obtain and develop these qualities, the rider has to reassure the horse and control the rhythm and balance of his movement. Even in the developing stage, the horse should never be allowed to drag his feet in walk; he should always lift his feet clear of the ground and place them accurately at every step. The biggest goal is to get a horse correctly straight on a straight line, and following exactly the curve of a circle, whatever its diameter.

The walk of a young horse is influenced by his relative lack of strength and understanding.

At the corners

Each corner is ridden as a quarter of a circle. The young horse does not bend naturally at the corners, so he has to be taught. To bend the horse, proceed in the following manner: corners should not be ridden too deep to start with. The horse must learn to take weight behind, and gradually develop collection.

- Move the horse's shoulders away from the wall during the straight line, keeping your rein contact equal and turning your shoulders slightly inward (shoulder-fore).

- When reaching the corner, use the bending aids:

  - Indicate the bend with the inside rein by opening it a little.

  - Drive the horse's outside shoulder and asking with the inside leg, toward the corner by opening the outside hand toward the wall, keeping a very focused contact with the horse's mouth, but not too strong a contact.

  - At the same time, be careful to keep the horse's bend by keeping his nose inwards with the inside rein if the horse does not react so well to the leg aids.

  - Simultaneously tap the horse's inside shoulder with a schooling whip.

  - Help maintain the bend and keep the horse active by using your inside leg at the girth.

  - Stop the haunches from escaping, controlling them with your outside rein and leg moved approximately one or two hands' width behind the girth.

  - Keep your shoulders parallel to the horse's shoulders, which puts a little more weight onto the inside seat bone. Be careful to sit still in the saddle.

Everything is a matter of balance and tactfulness. Maintain your aids without using strength, which would stiffen the horse.

The circle at walk

The work on a circle is the next logical stage. If each corner is a quarter of a circle, think of the circle as four quarter turns! Keep your bending aids and work on circles – decreasing and increasing the size to help the horse to develop in suppleness and responsiveness to the aids.

The essential goal is to keep the horse on the inside and outside aids. At this early stage with a young horse, do not hesitate to work with your hands well spread.

Ride every circle exactly round, with the same curve from the beginning to the end. It is impossible to relax, keep your rhythm or to put your horse on the bit if the circle is hesitant or badly described. If the parameters change constantly for the horse, he is going to stiffen, twist, hold back or run, depending on his personality.

Improving the walk starts with maintaining rhythm, fluency and accuracy.

Little by little, the horse will relax and have a free walk. The placement on the bit will then be possible, the neck will find its place and the hind end will become active. The beginning of a correct walk is born.

In time, voltes, demi-voltes and serpentines will maintain and renew the horse's attention. Lateral work, work in-hand, transitions, lengthening, work outside, halts and rein-back will progressively bring your horse to the school walk.

EXERCISES TO FURTHER DEVELOP THE WALK

Shoulder-in and half-pass

Corners, circles and shoulder-in are all of the same family of exercises. The shoulder-in, by lowering the haunches, and ensuring the haunches work in the direction of the forehand, will improve suppleness and submission. It is a fundamental building block you cannot ignore in obtaining a good walk. Provided that you address them at the correct time and in the correct sequence, do not hesitate to use all the different lateral exercises (see later in this book) in all possible variations. If you do this correctly, the compliance and relaxation of your horse will allow you to get closer to the ideal. However, if you ask too much, too hard, too often, you will discourage your horse, contract him and finally stop his progress in walk or any other gait. The horse must understand what is required both physically and mentally.

The work in-hand

Simultaneously with ridden exercises, well-conducted work in-hand (see previous chapter) will help to improve the walk. Without the weight of the rider (important for the young horse), it is possible to put the horse on the bit, to relax him, to go through the corners with the correct bend, to engage him in the shoulder-in and to obtain a good rhythm.

A calm, active extended walk
is the product of correct
progression in training.

RIGHT
Preparation and aids
for lengthening
the walk.

(left) The rider prepares the horse by asking for more energy.
(right) Giving the aids: the rider moves the contact forward
and down, relaxes the abdomen and the legs.

Collected, medium and extended walk and free walk on a loose rein contact

At an early stage, you just let your horse lengthen his stride freely between exercises or on straight lines, with the neck line open, relaxing both his muscles and his mind. When the horse stays in good posture, without difficulty, in an active, relaxed walk, it is time to ask for variations in the gait.

To start asking progressively for lengthening of the walk:

- First raise the quality of the walk (more energy, relaxation, better posture, more attention from the horse) and the degree of forward thrust, or 'impulsion'.

- Move your contact (meaning your hands, with the horse's mouth following) gradually forward allowing free movement of the horse's neck.

- Grow taller to allow your upper body to go with the horse's movement.

- Keep a light contact with your legs by using them alternately (right leg when the left foreleg of the horse goes forward, and vice versa).

- Do not try to push hard with your legs during the lengthening, rather concentrate on the preparation.

- Your horse has to keep his poll flexed and stay in a basically rounded outline, while lengthening his neck in varying degrees.

Transitions

The quality of a gait or of an exercise always determines the quality of the next gait or exercise. Therefore, the quality of the walk is an essential element that directly determines the quality of the trot or the canter that follows.

Perform frequent upward transitions (walk/trot, walk/canter) and downward transitions (trot/walk, canter/walk); they keep the horse attentive. They also demand straightness and submission, because he must stay active and ready to respond to your requests. (This is especially true of the canter/walk transition, which is illustrated in How to Improve the Canter in Chapter 7.)

During your transition, make sure of the following:

- The horse stays quiet and attentive, in the same frame of mind.

- The transition stays fluid.

- The poll is always the highest point, in the same place, without being stiff.

- The general balance stays the same.

- The actions of your upper torso, weight aids, hands and legs are never hard, but smooth and relaxed. Always ride the horse forwards to the hand first before the transition.

- The horse must take weight behind in a transition and develop collection.

Here again, the secret is in the preparation and in the rider's tact.

The walk outdoors

Your horse continues to 'learn' how to walk, how to shorten and lengthen his stride and to carry himself. You should work on this thoughtfully. You try to feel, to be precise. Ride out in the countryside. Go at first with another experienced horse, who moves well at the walk. Ride on flat ground first, then up and down hills, mostly at the walk and calmly. His walk will be irregular, sometimes hesitant. However, with continuing work, both in the arena and outdoors, confidence will come quickly.

Young horses benefit from being ridden outdoors in company.

ABOVE
Walking out well
through a meadow.

Sometimes it is good to
allow a horse freedom
in the walk. Here, free
walk on a long rein,
with good activity of
the hind legs.

With all the work in walk, be attentive, always have a correct horse, in the correct bend. Most of the time, try to put him on the bit ('in your hand'), even outdoors. Watch the regularity and the rhythm of the strides. In short, continue to educate his walk. However, sometimes, also, let him walk on a long rein – allowing the contact forwards and downwards, stretching through the body.

THE HALT FROM THE WALK

With the very young horse, keep it simple by asking him to stand still by the wall.

Even at the walk, you can teach the beginning of collection by asking for the halt on a contact in a novice outline – in front of the vertical.

To halt, proceed as follows:

- Raise the quality of the walk.

- Stretch up tall in your upper body, lower your shoulders, push your hips forward.

- Close your fingers without hardness.

- Because of the movement of your upper torso, your hands will raise slightly.

- Keep your legs in contact. The legs close, to ask the horse to step under his centre of gravity.

The aids for halt from walk.

(left) Giving the aids: the rider stretches up through the body, lowers the shoulders and pushes the hips forward. The fingers are closed softly. The legs are kept in contact.

(right) When the horse is at halt, the rider plays softly with the fingers to relax the horse's jaw and neck.

- When the horse is at halt, play softly with your fingers to relax his jawand neck.

- To go forward into walk, relax your hands, and with your legs softly in contact, allow the forward movement with your upper body.

- Be less demanding at the beginning, then later ask progressively for more engagement of the haunches, and sustain a well-framed halt for longer.

- Vary the places where you ask for halt, and the exercises you do before and after a halt.

In due course, the transitions walk to halt can be improved by riding the halt from half-pass (A) and shoulder-in (B).

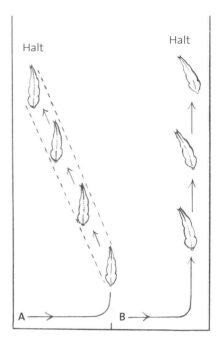

A balanced, square halt.

REIN-BACK

The rein-back is a very useful exercise that encourages the horse to pick up his hind feet and bring them under his haunches. In order to go backwards correctly, the horse must remain straight: rein-back improves straightness, collection and 'throughness'.

In rein-back, the legs do not move in the four-time sequence of walk, but in a two-time diagonal sequence akin to trot.

How to ride rein-back

When the halt is correctly framed, soft, with the horse straight, light, his neck and jaw relaxed, then the horse is ready to rein-back.

Proceed as follows:

- Give a very light and very brief indication with your legs.

- Lighten by moving your upper torso very slightly forward.

- 'Carry' your wrists, close your fingers for an instant.

- As the horse begins a step backward, let your fingers relax and cease the forwards driving leg aid, reward...

- Start again and ask more, progressively.

- When the horse steps back, the aids practically cease – just follow with your fingers and control the straightness.

- Everything is a question of feel and balance of your upper torso.

- Reining-back correctly is like walking correctly. It requires regularity, equal strides, rhythm and lightness.

The sequence of footfall in rein-back.

Rein-back.

BELOW
The aids for rein-back.

(left) From a square, relaxed halt, the rider gives a light indication with the legs, moves the chest forward slightly and closes the fingers for an instant. (centre) As the first step back is achieved, the rider relaxes the fingers...
(right) ...and asks again.

- The horse's neck stays at the same height. The horse is straight, the haunches are controlled.

- Following the rein-back, always send your horse forward smoothly – never roughly or abruptly – and without movement of the neck.

THE SCHOOL WALK

School walk is a very slow walk which is extremely useful for training purposes as it gives both horse and rider time to correct technique. It is different to collected walk. The horse does not take more weight behind, as it would in a collected walk, but it is simply slower and in a clear rhythm.

What to look for in the school walk

- A very slow walk, without asking for more collection

- A balanced horse, with slow but active hind legs and haunches, with sufficient weight behind to remain balanced

- A horse retains a supple back and is relaxed in his attitude.

- The neck arches forwards from the withers and is carried with the poll the highest point.

- Free-moving shoulders.

- The steps of the horse do not shorten in length, they just slow down. Working slowly gives the rider time to train the horse, and gives the horse time to understand.

The particular characteristics of the school walk are absence of resistance, soft contact, quiet mouth, and the footfalls touching the ground delicately. It requires total submission of the horse.

How to obtain the school walk

- By working on the quality of the horse's walk patiently and methodically.

- By seeking balance, dynamism, roundness, rhythm all in a relaxed manner, to get closer to the ideal walk.

- By trying to obtain a slow walk to allow the horse to take correct steps to improve his movement,

- Take particular care of your posture: sit deeply, in a perfect position, relaxed.

The school walk develops the qualities mentioned above.

Collected walk – in school walk the horse would have a more relaxed head carriage.

MY ADVICE ON THE WALK

- Each horse has his own walk, his interior music.

- Feel what the rhythm of your horse's walk is.

- When your horse walks relaxed, in the right rhythm, with forward thrust, you will know that the tempo is the right one.

- When lengthening the walk strides, retain the contact with your horse's mouth; maintain his head-carriage with the poll the highest point but he must be allowed to lengthen his frame.

- Follow and amplify the lengthened strides with your seat and push very little with your legs, because they sometimes make the horse lose rhythm.

- The walk is not a mechanical problem: do not try to analyse the mechanics of the walk… rather try to feel whether your horse is in tune, that he is not changing his speed, his rhythm, or his posture.

- Do not ask your horse anything difficult before he can walk in a relaxed manner, in good posture and with forward thrust.

- The horse must be freely 'forward' without being held back – he is simply in the channel set by your aids.

- The height of the poll and of the forehand arises from a visible lowering of the haunches, not the opposite – do not forget that!

- When riding at walk, you should prefer to have a poll that is too low rather than one that is too high, because the latter stiffens the horse and hollows his back.

- Have a light horse, but do not completely 'let go'.

- At the walk, two dangers await the rider: limpness and agitation (abandonment and excess of control) – do not fall into either one!

- To have a straight horse along a wall, take the shoulders slightly in from the wall, because the shoulders are a little narrower than the haunches.

- Every now and then, take the inside track or the centre line to check the quality of your walk and the straightness of your horse and his obedience to your aids.

- Take care of your posture – the quality of your walk depends on it!

- When walking, use your legs sparingly: act little but at the right moment; do not squeeze with your legs.

- Release the muscles of your back, simply support your lower back.

- You must push and slow down with your back, without moving your seat.

- Command your horse with your upper torso, the rest is secondary!

- Follow the walk of your horse with your abdomen and upper torso, not with your hands.

- Look for a fluid, regular, and very even contact between mouth and hands.

- Have very soft hands, light, supple, especially during lengthening and shortening of the stride, during transitions, and while bending and changing the bend.

- Try not to slow down, not to 'turn off' the horse, but just to channel his energy.

- Do not let your horse put weight in your hands.

- When the horse is on the bit, in rhythm, practise reducing the effects of your hands and your legs (the *descente de main et de jambes* described in Chapter 2).

- Riding corners in walk helps to develop collection.

- On a circle, with a young horse, do not hesitate to form a triangle between your hands and the horse's mouth – spread your hands.

- Frequently increase and decrease the size of your circles. (Ride leg yield as you increase, for example.)

- Make sure every circle is round and accurate.

- To go from one circle to another, keep your attention on the change of bend.

- Slightly relax your fingers, play with your fingers to lower the horse's neck slightly: you will gain fluidity.

- On straight lines between the circles, relax your fingers just a fraction: your horse will keep the same position; he will relax too.

- In a walk transition, look for fluidity, with no abruptness, no excess of reaction, and no limpness. Every transition should be well executed.

- Before any transition, slightly lower your horse's neck and check your forwardness.

- Stay relaxed yourself – do not tense up, as this will affect your horse.

- If you want to halt your horse, count down the desired number of strides before stopping, this will make the preparation easier.

- Never rein-back using strength: never rein-back when the horse is resisting.

- When reining-back, think about the famous maxim, and re-apply it: 'calm, backward, straight'.

- Also, work on reining-back in-hand, slowly, along the wall, with the schooling whip parallel to the horse's body, to prevent the haunches from stepping inside into the arena.

- In-hand, be very smooth and economical with the actions of your hand: move your upper body back; determine how many steps you want your horse to take back, then carry him forward with tact.

FREQUENTLY ENCOUNTERED PROBLEMS IN WALK

Should I always start working at the walk?

- It is best to start with a good workout on the lunge, at the trot mostly, then you can get on your horse and start walking.

- With some very energetic, generous horses, it is better to start working at the trot, always calmly, and then work at the walk. However, generally, a good schooling session starts with a good-quality walk.

- Once the horse gives everything you require of him at the walk and is relaxed, attentive and responsive, do not wait, do not bore your horse: take the trot. You have to feel the right moment.

How long should I work at the walk?

- There are no absolute rules. You must, however, develop a feeling for the quantity of walk to give to your horse, and then trot at the right moment.

- A stiff or nervous horse has to work longer at the walk: you will only trot when your horse is relaxed, loose, regular. Then, walk again to check that your horse has stayed calm. This work can take half of your schooling time.

- With a less energetic horse, who has a tendency to 'fall asleep' during the walk, you will trot sooner and then alternate short periods of walk/trot, trot/walk, walk/canter, canter/walk…

- The young horse needs to walk for a fairly long time, until he is calm, attentive, submissive. It will then be easier to channel his energy at the faster gaits.

- The length of time at the walk is also determined by the degree of training of the horse, and by the goal established before each schooling session.

My horse is not straight

This is a response to a query from a pupil who said: 'The left hind leg of my mare steps to the left and, on the left rein, she often puts her haunches in. Is it possible to correct this problem with the right set of exercises, and if yes, what should I do?'

- Your mare is not 'straight'. She 'crosses over', meaning that her haunches do not follow the axis of direction; they come inside to escape your control or refuse to engage.

- Your posture on the horse might be off balance. Spread your weight better, make sure you are equally on your two seat bones.

- Maybe your aids are not symmetrical. If so, balance them. Too much inside rein, too much bend or a neck angled toward the inside twists a horse. The horse then leans on that rein by becoming harder, 'sticks to the inside leg' and places the haunches to the inside. Use less inside rein, but do not abandon the contact on the outside rein.

- It could be that the mare has difficulty using her haunches to the left, that she has a bad, crooked posture, in which case a thorough gymnastic workout should help put her on the correct axis. Work on shoulder-in/shoulder-fore at the three gaits on a straight line and on a circle. This will take her shoulders away from the wall and will supple and engage her inside hind leg. This exercise will correct the inside hind leg from stepping to the left and teach the horse to move away from, not against, the inside leg.

- Also work on circles on the left rein, as an exercise, and make her put her haunches out. Work on straight lines with a touch of shoulder-in.

- These exercises will put your mare straight, so that she will move on one single line, the shoulders in front of the haunches, with no bend.

- Finally, good impulsion will make her stretch out and put the haunches back behind the line of the shoulders. If your mare is holding back, she will have the tendency to traverse (step over).

Voila…what you can do to straighten your mare…

Crookedness in rein-back; the hind leg stepping out.

My horse does not rein-back straight

- He is not correctly framed, the action of one leg or hand is stronger than the other.

- You must realign the shoulders and the haunches of the horse with an opposing rein, to straighten him. This must be done with no abruptness, but with suppleness, within two to three steps.

- As soon as the horse is straight again, take another two to three steps back, halt and ride him forward.

- Start reining-back again, being particularly careful: reward.

Difficulty in placing a young horse on the bit

- This is a response to a query from a pupil who owned of a 4½-year-old horse. She said: 'I currently have to resolve a problem that will condition the entirety of my work: it is putting the horse on the bit; the stability of the placement of my horse. I manage it initially at the walk, but he does not stay on the bit because my technique is uncertain…' This is an example of the value of using walk as the basic training gait.

- Your horse is young. It is of utmost importance to put him in the right posture, on the bit, and in a stable and relaxed manner.

- To place a horse (put him on the bit) is not the result of tricks, miracle recipes, mechanical actions of the hands or any other miscellaneous means used by all kinds of people. It is the result of the general balance of the horse, of his forward thrust, of the engagement of the hindquarters and of his relaxation.

- To place your horse better and with more stability, look to all those matters as a priority.

- Work your horse on the lunge at the trot. After he is warmed up, use the side reins to place him gradually and progressively in the correct posture.

- Do several schooling sessions just on the lunge and always lunge before riding.

- Since your horse is young, do not ask for the poll to be too high, but find the position in which he feels good, and relaxes.

- Feel, think … frame your horse well in the channel of the aids.

- Take care of the bend on circles.

- Pay much attention to your posture. A horse cannot place his head correctly if the rider is not in balance and relaxed.

- Keep your hands still, just above the withers – above all do not try to use the right hand, left hand, right hand… making the horse's head swing.

- Do not move your hands, but play with your fingers.

- Steady your inside hand and use your outside hand more, but softly.

- Keep your legs relaxed but attentive.

- Work a lot on circles and half-circles.

- At the change of bend, make your horse lower his poll: you will see that your horse will start to come on the bit.

- Act with softness, do not ask much, and keep him in a rather low position.

- The shoulder-in will help.

First, ask him to come on the bit in walk and trot – establish it – at the canter, let him be relatively free for the moment, in a slightly open position, but always in balance. This is how you put a horse on the bit!

CHAPTER SIX

THE TROT

As with walk, the first priority with trot is to look for the purity of the gait. Only after he trots with harmony, relaxation and rhythm, in a correct posture, round, light and energetic, can the horse start on the harder exercises building on the development of the trot, and leading to passage and piaffe.

The trot is a diagonal gait with two beats, with a period of suspension in between. If walk is the gait of apprenticeship, the trot is the perfect gait to allow the development of rhythm.

PURPOSES OF WORKING AT TROT

Working at the trot has several purposes:

- It improves the range and the regularity of the strides.

- It muscles and strengthens the horse.

- It supples the joints.

- It develops communication between horse and rider.

- It gives the horse better balance and rhythm.

- It develops collection.

The sequence of
footfall at trot.

Working at the trot is of fundamental importance for the training of the horse. The rider must give it great attention and always try to improve it. Points to look for in a good trot are:

- An equal and symmetrical push of each hind leg.

- A great regularity in the touchdown of the diagonals.

- A rigorously equal distance between each step.

- An equal range and elevation of each leg, the same movement at each stride.

Close attention to these four criteria will develop rhythm until it reaches perfection.

The trot can only be good if the horse is totally relaxed, mentally and physically; fluid, with a constant balance and posture. In a good trot the horse is on the bit without stiffness, the shoulders are free, the actions of the legs are supple, and the 'impulsion' (the forward thrust), is regular. The horse carries himself straight in the shoulders and the haunches, with no twisting, stretched out by the impulsion, ready for any change in direction or gait.

The daily development of these qualities will take the young horse toward collected trot, and eventually to the refinement of the school trot and the airs above the ground.

HOW TO IMPROVE A YOUNG HORSE'S TROT

The young horse, bothered by the weight of the rider, very often trots irregularly, in a semblance of horizontal balance, his neck rather low, in an open posture, with the angle of his head/neck open. He hollows his back, speeds up or slows down at the merest movement of the rider, worries easily, often deviates from his path, and bends toward the outside in the corners.

At this stage, your most important goal is to develop the horse's back. This will help to avoid sudden accelerations and to obtain regular strides of trot, well-framed in the channel of the aids.

Work on the lunge in trot

Working on the lunge is the best way to start developing muscles without the weight of the rider, to relax and balance the horse in trot, to regularize the trot in a correct posture, and to make him comfortable. Thus it can be seen that lunge lessons are just as important to the training of the horse as the mounted lessons.

The trot of a young horse: a semblance of horizontal balance, his neck rather low, with the angle of his head/neck fairly open.

First, you must lunge your horse a couple of minutes on each rein with long side reins at the trot to relax him and to loosen up the muscles.

Be careful! As I mentioned in the chapter on lungeing, the lunge rein is never attached to the rings of the bit, but *always* – I insist – to the lunge cavesson, to avoid any injury to the horse's mouth arising from resistance or 'jumps of joy'.

After the initial warm-up, start using simple soft leather side reins. These are attached laterally to the roller or the girth, just below the flaps of the saddle, and to the rings of the bit. The rein on the inside will be around 3 to 5 holes shorter, to bend the horse on the circle. The side reins must be adjusted so that the horse is positioned correctly with a light contact to the bit, the head being just in front of the vertical. The horse must keep a certain freedom of his head whilst being almost on the bit, but he must not be pulled into position or provoked into fighting the side reins.

The details of work on the lunge are given in Chapter 4. A summary of the main points as they relate to trot work with a young horse are as follows.

The horse is well framed between the 'hand' (the lunge rein) and the 'legs' (the long whip, the aid to forward thrust). The hand controls him with slight vibrations of the lunge rein; the whip determines the impulsion with discreet, precise and perfectly controlled actions.

Work on each rein for intervals of between five and ten minutes (depending on the energy, the muscle mass and the training of the horse), looking mainly for regularity of the trot and consistency of impulsion. Progressively ask for as much impulsion as possible while keeping a relaxed horse.

Try to feel the correct rhythm for the horse.

This work will allow your horse to develop stronger muscles, to stretch out his topline, to make his trot more regular, and to find his balance without the weight of the rider.

Rising trot

The young horse is still lacking strength under saddle. He cannot properly support a rider on his back for very long and he stiffens quickly when trotting.

Therefore, at first, almost all trot work must be done at the rising trot to relieve the horse's back every other stride, allowing both horse and rider to be comfortable. However, you need to know how to rise to the trot with suppleness and in balance. The following is a summary of how trot correctly on (in this example) the left diagonal:

- Shorten your stirrup leathers one or two holes.

- Shorten your reins slightly.

- Carry your upper torso forward a little and let the left diagonal lift you a couple of inches off the saddle, while you put your weight on the stirrups, with your legs (between the knee and the heel) stretched down, the heels down placed on a line vertically beneath the seat bones.

- At the moment the left diagonal touches the ground, let yourself fall softly back into the saddle.

- Rise again when the left diagonal rises again.

- Keep an even contact with the horse's mouth, the reins adjusted softly, without moving you hands.

- You must keep the same forward position of your upper torso, the same balance and the same rhythm for each stride.

- It is essential not to interfere with the horse in his trot.

- If the stride is big and very energetic, your upper torso must be inclined a little forward.

- On the other hand, the more the trot is collected, the more you straighten up (torso becomes more vertical).

- On a bend, in a corner or on a circle, (to the right, for example) the outside diagonal travels a longer distance than the inside diagonal. By rising with the outside (left) diagonal, you trigger a slight forward push of this left diagonal and therefore allow it to travel a bit further than the right diagonal. The horse will then be able to keep an even rhythm on the circle.

When the horse starts to get a better balance and rhythm, you can start to sit in the saddle, your lower back in tune with the horse's movement. However, if the young horse starts to hold back a little, return to rising trot before his back starts to hollow.

Rising trot: the rider's seat is eased softly from the saddle on one diagonal and returns softly on the next.

Sitting trot

As stated, you can start to introduce short periods of sitting trot when the horse is showing signs of strengthening up and can trot in good rhythm and balance.

In sitting trot, the rider's seat does not drive down into the saddle – the rider sits softly in balance with the horse:

- The two seat bones stay in contact with the saddle, without moving.

- The seat simply goes with the motion, passively, without trying to push the horse, which only tightens the horse's back.

- The lower back stays supple in natural posture, depending on how the rider is built.

Areas to be relaxed when sitting to the trot.

- The legs hang lightly against the horse's sides.

- The legs should avoid gripping (if the legs, knees, or the calves become tense, the rider will become tight in the hips).

- The upper torso stays close to the vertical, relaxed with no stiffness (this is impossible if the legs are tense).

- The arms are slightly bent, and hang naturally against the upper body from the shoulder.

- The hands should be as quiet as possible and carried just above the saddle.

In short, the softness of the seat, the suppleness of the lower back, the position of the upper body and the contact with the horse's mouth will be determined by how relaxed the rider is and how well they have learnt to sit.

The rider's posture will define the balance, the size of the strides, the rhythm and the relaxation of the horse's trot.

Looking for cadence

First, it is necessary to distinguish between rhythm and cadence – they are not one and the same thing. Rhythm relates to regularity, but regularity itself can be good or bad. For example, a horse who trots with stiff steps with his hind legs out behind him, but does so with regularity, is moving rhythmically, but the trot is a poor one. The rhythm is correct when the horse moves with ease, in a stable and balanced posture, active and relaxed at the same time. The horse feels good and works with pleasure; the rider is relaxed, stable, and can work without tiring.

Even assuming that the basic rhythm is good, every horse has his own rhythm in a trot – the hard part is to find the correct cadence. To do this, first find the best possible posture for the horse: more or less on the bit, neck more or less elevated, degree of bend controlled in the circles…

It is for you to feel and choose what balance to give your horse. Start with minimal forward thrust (impulsion), go with the essential relaxation of the trot. When the horse is on the bit and relaxed, progressively ask for more impulsion. If the horse stiffens or becomes unbalanced, that means you are asking for too much. Then, you must ask for a little less, to find the requisite degree of impulsion with which the horse can remain balanced and relaxed.

When your horse feels good and does not alter anything in his balance, his impulsion or his posture on the circles and changes of bend, whether at the sitting or rising trot, you have found the cadence that suits your horse. You can validate this by reducing the effects of your hands and your legs, as described in Chapter 2. The horse should be able to carry himself in the trot without your rein aids.

Exercises to improve the trot

Session after session, the horse develops his rhythm, the size of his strides and the roundness of his back. You must take particular care of the work on circles, the voltes, the corners, and the changes of bend on the serpentines. The underlying 'philosophy' and the way to proceed have been described in the chapter on The Walk (Improving the Walk).

Shoulder-in and half-passes must be executed with tact in a correct, rhythmical and relaxed manner. The exercises should be varied: travers (head to the wall), renvers (croup to the wall) and shoulder-in and half-pass are unrivalled exercises to confirm and develop the trot toward collected trot. Also – spiralling in and out on circles is very effective. Advice on the way to proceed, and dealing with the problems encountered, is given in Chapter 9.

The trot outdoors

Do not hesitate to work on your trot outdoors, on good flat or slightly hilly terrain. Be very attentive. Keep your horse on the bit, on the correct bend and in balance. Watch the regularity of the trot and the degree of the horse's relaxation. If your horse stays in balance and in rhythm, let him stretch forwards and downwards into a long rein.

A lot of people riding outdoors sit too long to the trot – what a mistake! They get tired and the horse's back is overworked for no reason. The rising trot, on the other hand, relieves the horse and allows the strides to become longer. The rider is in balance on the stirrups, the upper torso moves more or less forward depending on the rhythm of the trot, and the hands remain still, lightly against the withers.

Another common error is to trot too fast, or for too long. A generous horse will end up hollowing his back, and will ruin his hocks or damage his joints. There again, you must find the right rhythm. You can trot with a somewhat

An onward-bound trot outdoors, with the horse showing an easy inclination to lengthen his stride.

bigger stride and more energy, but always, I repeat, always, in balance, and working over the back with active hindquarters, through to the horse's mouth, and back to the rider's hand.

Lengthening, leading to extension of the trot

While working on the transitions halt/trot/halt, walk/trot/walk and trot/canter/trot, try to shorten and lengthen your horse's steps. Note that rhythm must be maintained when shortening or lengthening the stride: irregularities of rhythm will have adverse effects on the desired length of steps.

The extended trot is the result of impulsion added in the collection. Without needing to be pushed, the horse sends his forelegs forward, the extension starting at the shoulder and finishing at the tip of the hoof, and the back staying flexible. The hind legs are engaged forcefully under the weight of the horse and leave the ground very clearly. The size of the strides, the suppleness, the balance and the rhythm define a beautiful extension in the trot.

Stiffness, quickening, uneven extensions and imbalance on the shoulders are not part of a well-understood method, but just a contest of strength.

Full extension of the trot is built upon teaching the horse to lengthen progressivly. Here is how to proceed:

- Clearly ask for more collection and a more energetic, forward-thinking trot, on a circle, or on a shoulder-in on the circle, and/or on the short side of the arena.

- Obtain extra impulsion, with bigger steps (more ground cover) but without speeding up.

- In the strides preceding the lengthened trot, your hands are very still and keep the horse well on the bit.

- Straighten up and progressively place the horse's shoulders at the beginning of the diagonal or on the long side of the arena.

- Carry your contact with the horse's mouth (hand/mouth) forward and down and let your horse lengthen.

- Push with your abdomen, your buttocks and your back, doing almost nothing with your legs.

Medium trot: the defined length of stride between working and extended trot.

Extended trot – the rider allowing the horse to lengthen his frame.

- During the lengthened strides, retain the contact with your horse's mouth; don't let him lose his head-carriage. (Particularly at the medium trot, the horse has to stay well on the bit.)

- Follow and amplify the lengthened strides with your seat and push very little with your legs, because they sometimes make the horse lose his rhythm.

THE SCHOOL TROT

School trot is a very slow trot which is extremely useful for training purposes as it gives both horse and rider time to correct technique. It differs from collected trot, in that the rhythm is slower, but the horse does not take more weight behind, as it would in collected trot. The two are very different.

The school trot is just that – for schooling. In competition, you would use collected trot, where you would want the horse to take weight behind.

  The school trot requires:

- Maintain the horse's correct outline, with the poll the highest point and the neck forwards from the withers.

- Focused, slower movements from the horse.

- A slow and majestic cadence.

- Keep the horse absolutely straight.

- A total absence of stiffness.

- The jaw yields to the soft action of the rider's fingers.

Collected trot – the neck here is higher than in a school trot.

- The joints should move in a relaxed manner, the shoulders move freely and the hind legs sufficiently engaged just to maintain balance.

- The relaxation of the horse is total, and the balance is so good that you can reduce the effects of your hands and your legs for long periods of time.

The school trot is obtained by asking for a slow trot which day by day, strengthens and exercises all the joints, the muscles, and develops suppleness.

Circles, lateral work, the transitions trot/halt/rein-back/trot, the shortening and extension of the trot, and the variations of the rhythm are the key exercises to progressively improving the trot.

The school trot is helpful as preparation for the horse for collected work in the trot, which can later develop into advanced movements such as piaffe and passage.

MY ADVICE ON THE TROT

General points

- Do not forget: trot is, above all, the search for regularity, cadence and roundness. You dream of a horse perfectly on the bit, with a beautiful head-carriage, the poll high…very well!… but it is sometimes better to work the trot with a lower poll, even a low neck, while very relaxed. (I do not say behind the bit!) When the poll is high, and it does not result from a clear engagement of the hindquarters but just from the rider's hand actions, the horse will only hollow his back and strain his hocks.

- If you kick the horse's sides constantly with your heels, you will destroy your horse's trot. Keep your legs soft, act little and at the right moment, with fast and light touches.

- When trotting, do not oppose the forward thrust: the rider must have the feeling that the horse is taking him forwards willingly. The hands act like a filter. Let the necessary amount of energy through.

- Precede all hand actions with an action of your upper torso and legs it is the most efficient way to balance and regularize the trot. Push and slow down with your back, not with your hands.

The left-hand picture shows a horse with a slightly lowered poll and neck, working in a relaxed but forward-thinking way. This is much preferable to an outline in which the poll and neck are raised as a result of the rider's hand actions, rather than from true engagement of the hindquarters – a posture which stresses the back and hocks and impedes true forward movement.

- Between the horse's mouth and the rider's hands, there is a contact that is soft, fluid, regular, and equal when the horse is in balance, and trots in self-carriage.

- Do not forget to reduce the aids with your hands and your legs (*descente de main et de jambes*). The horse should respond to light aids.

With a young horse

- With a young horse, alternate rising and sitting trot. Try to feel when the horse needs to be relieved from your weight on his back. Also, do not sit too deeply in the saddle. Have a lighter seat. Let your back absorb the motion. You may sit more vertically once your horse's collection progresses.

- On a circle with a young horse, carry your hands one fist's height above the withers, and do not hesitate to spread your hands if difficulties appear. If

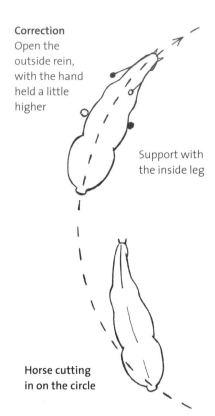

Correction
Open the outside rein, with the hand held a little higher

Support with the inside leg

Horse cutting in on the circle

Correcting a horse cutting in on a circle in trot.

your horse tries to cut in towards the inside of the circle, *open* your outside rein and *support with your inside leg.* (Do not just pull on the outside rein, as some riders do.)

Rising trot

- The essential at the rising trot is that you are in balance, with a natural, supple movement, in tune with your horse. Outdoors, change diagonal every now and then, so that you do not tire one diagonal more than the other.

Sitting trot

- At the sitting trot, keep your buttocks relaxed, your legs down, in order to have a light back – not the opposite!

- Your seat bones and your buttocks should not move excessively. The hips should be pressed slightly forwards.

- Your lower back should be straight, but with no stiffness and absolutely not rounded or slouching.

The cadence

- When trotting, always control the rhythm. No rhythm, no beauty.

- Every horse has his own cadence, his 'interior music': feel the music of your horse and let him express himself.

- While looking for the right cadence, be careful not to confuse slowness with laziness, or speed with impulsion – it will be a big mistake

- Lots of horses go too fast when trotting: they stiffen, their stride shortens and they lose relaxation. They progress very little. Check if you should not slow your trot down, without changing your impulsion: look for elastic, rhythmic and powerful steps.

Impulsion (forward thrust)

- Please your horse by letting him put all the energy and joy he can into his trot. Simply control his balance and his posture and above all… never let him lose his relaxation and rhythm.

- Look for the optimum forward thrust that lets the horse stay relaxed, keeps the stride at its biggest and the movement forwards and working over the back.

- Do not confuse impulsion and speed.

- At the trot, you must first seek balance and relaxation in order to allow impulsion to develop. It is much more efficient this way, less tiring than squeezing with your legs at every stride. If you constantly keep your legs or your spurs on the horse he will hold back and become tense. Instead, apply fast touches with a soft leg.

- Impulsion in the trot (and in all the other gaits) results from the horse's frame of mind – a desire to carry himself forward.

- Know how to alternate resting periods, trotting periods, and walking periods. Also know when to trot with your horse on the bit and rounded, or trot with long reins.

- The essential is to preserve a good balance, an equal rhythm, to have good control and to allow the horse to stretch forwards and downwards when the reins are lengthened.

Transitions

- In the transitions walk/trot and trot/canter always prepare your horse well, e.g. cantering in a corner is easiest for a horse to understand.

- Never go from trot to canter on a circle if the horse is not perfectly bent and on the aids.

Lengthened strides

- At the medium trot the horse should lengthen his frame.

- At the extended trot, allow the horse to put his nose forwards, follow and drive with your lower back – simply let your hands go in the direction of the horse's mouth, forward and down.

- Ask the horse to lengthen with strong leg aids – just make sure always to increase the impulsion before asking for lengthened steps.

Collected trot

- Try to win in height what you lose in length to collect your horse.

- Collect your horse progressively. Win a thousandth of a collection every-day and you will obtain the collected trot in three years! A little joke, but think about it!

FREQUENTLY ENCOUNTERED PROBLEMS IN TROT

I cannot find balance and rhythm in a rising trot

Your are behind or ahead of the horse: probably because you make an effort to rise, you raise your shoulders, and you are falling back in your saddle at the wrong time.

As mentioned in Chapter 3 of this book, the most common fault in novice riders is rising too high out of the saddle, making an actual effort to do so and throwing the body upwards from the knees. The correct method is to *allow* the horse's momentum to push the pelvis out of the saddle: the hips should move forwards towards the hands. In this way there will be no gripping with your legs, or tension in your calves and knees; you will be relaxed through the legs, which can then be quietly 'wrapped around' the horse. Instead of landing heavily, your seat will drop softly into the saddle and because your upper body will not be moving up and down your hands will be still and steady.

Lessons on the lunge can be valuable in helping you to achieve the correct action.

My legs and feet move in rising trot

You are not in balance on top of your points of support. Your centre of gravity absolutely has to be vertical to your points of support – your two feet in the stirrups. Your heels have to be directly under your buttocks.

Try to rise off the saddle at halt, with your legs very forward or backward – it's impossible. Then, put your heels under your seat bones, put your upper torso slightly forward and you will rise with no effort. Once up, you will stay in balance. If you put your heels forward again, they will not be under your seat bones anymore and you will fall back heavily in the saddle. If you put your heels back, you will fall forward.

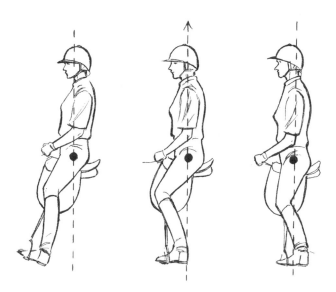

Correct and incorrect points of support in rising trot. In the left-hand picture, the rider's leg is too far forward. This rider may seek support from the reins in rising, and will fall back heavily whilst 'sitting'. The central picture shows a rider with correct heel/hip/ shoulder alignment. The right-hand picture shows a rider with heel too far back; this rider will tend to fall forwards whilst rising and will easily get out of rhythm with the horse's movement.

Then, do the same at trot. The heels down, exactly underneath the buttocks, the upper torso slightly forward. The horse will lift you up on one diagonal, and you will land in the saddle softly at the moment that diagonal re-touches the ground. You are in dynamic balance, you control your hands and your upper torso, and follow the horse's movement with suppleness.

I bounce in the saddle and I move at the sitting trot

If you bounce in the saddle, your hands, shoulders and upper torso move; you are stiff, your back is sore and you tire easily. On top of that, you prevent your horse from going forward, you hurt his back…he fights back or gives up.

And you have been working hard for months or years, you trot without stirrups, you try to do a sitting trot for longer and to relax your upper body… It is exhausting and useless! You are discouraged, you avoid the sitting trot!

You bounce and you move because you are supporting yourself with your thighs, your knees, and your calves…and the more you squeeze with them in order not to come off the saddle, the more you will stiffen up and the more you will bounce.

Simply relax your buttocks, your thighs, your calves and your heels… in very little time, you will have surprising results as you find harmony with your horse's movements.

It is sometimes difficult for a beginner, or a rider who had bad experiences, to deal with their fear and to relax physically, but the relaxation of the lower body also happens in your mind – one cannot work without the other!

Forging in extensions

This is a response to a query from a pupil who said: 'When I ask for extensions at the trot, my mare forges. What is the cause? How can I fix it?'

When a horse extends his trot distinctively, the hind legs hit the ground well in front of the prints of the forelegs. The toe of a hind leg can hit the heel or the ends of the shoe of the foreleg: the horse 'forges'. He can hurt his heels, or even sometimes pull off a front shoe.

Some horses have a tendency to forge, especially newly shod youngsters who lack balance and engagement, but also any other horses who are not in balance. Therefore, be very careful to keep your mare in balance on her haunches when extending the trot, with her hind legs well engaged.

The extension has to come from an increased impulsion and a strong engagement of the hind-quarters…not from a weight transfer to the horse's shoulders and a quickening of the strides.

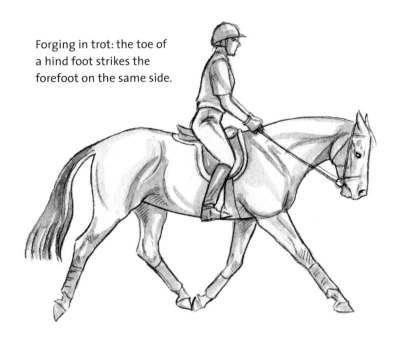

Forging in trot: the toe of a hind foot strikes the forefoot on the same side.

Keep the contact with your mare's mouth by taking it forward and down, but without letting her come off the bit and/or put herself on her shoulders.

The problem should disappear – if it continues, and you are sure that lack of balance is not the main cause, you can modify the shoeing of your mare. First, have the toe of the hind legs squared off ('square toe'). You can also have the ends of the front shoes shortened slightly. Talk to your farrier, but act carefully and progressively.

For extreme cases, like racing Trotters who amplify their strides a lot, they use modified shoes (the outside branch of the shoe is longer) to try to spread their hind legs.

But here, we are outside the subject of classical riding…

CHAPTER SEVEN

THE CANTER AND COUNTER-CANTER

The canter is a gait with three beats, in which the horse's legs hit the ground in the following order:

- One hind leg, first beat.

- One diagonal biped, second beat.

- The remaining foreleg, third beat.

- When the horse canters to the right, the sequence is left hind, right hind and left fore together, and right fore.

If the canter is correct, regardless of the phase of the stride cycle, the supporting legs should not be burdened unevenly. For example, in the diagonal phase, both the hind leg and its diagonally opposite foreleg should each bear half the weight. The leg sequence just described remains the same in all tempos. A canter becomes faulty when four hoof beats can be heard, when for example the inner hind foot is placed on the ground before the diagonal (outside) foreleg. In such cases (sometimes caused by incorrect collection) the horse loses impulsion and no longer canters forwards.

A high degree of true collection in the canter is the sign of good training. The horse moves with beauty, appears taller and is relaxed. The forehand becomes majestic, the hind end flexes. The rider's aids become invisible; the rider follows and supports the horse.

The sequence of foot-falls in canter: here, the horse is leading to the right.

The horse is moving with freedom and thus he can execute all the exercises: circles, serpentines, changes of lead, circles on two tracks, pirouettes and canter almost on the spot

To take a young horse towards a collected canter requires technique, patience and skill: it is a fascinating exercise.

THE AIDS FOR THE CANTER DEPART

There is a lot of controversy about this subject! Should one use diagonal or lateral aids? The outside or the inside rein or leg? Such debate misses the key point. When you ask for canter, the most important thing is to lighten and free the inside half of your horse. Acting with the inside or outside leg is mostly a matter of tact and timing.

The following is a summary of the basic aids for the canter depart:

- Support the outside shoulder of the horse with your outside rein and free the horse's inside shoulder.

- Keep the flexion with the inside rein.

- Put weight on both seat bones equally, with a bit more weight in the inside stirrup.

- Ask for the canter depart by putting your outside leg back so the heel is in line with the hip and touch the horse lightly.

- Keep your inside leg at the girth and use this leg *after* the canter strike off.

How do you do this with a very young horse? Shortly after his breaking in, the horse can canter very freely from the trot. He must now learn to canter at the rider's command together with voice and whip aids.

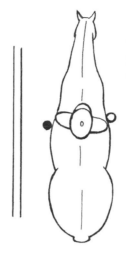

- Outside (left) rein supports the horse's outside shoulder and lightens the inside shoulder.

- Inside (right) rein keeps the flexion.

- Sit on both seat bones equally with weight slightly into inside stirrup.

- Outside (left) leg asks for canter depart behind the girth.

- Inside (right) leg remains at the girth and is used *after* the transition.

The aids for canter – in this example, to the right.

- Collect the trot a little more, start positioning your aids for the canter depart (outside leg and inside shoulder a little further back, weight on both seat bones and reins equally in contact).

- On the short side of the arena, just before the next corner, touch with your outside leg.

- At the same time, lightly touch the inside shoulder with a schooling whip and ask with your voice: 'canter'. (The horse knows the command from being lunged.)

- Ask for the canter depart on both reins.

- When the horse gives you an easy canter depart from trot, proceed in the same way from walk.

- Then, vary the place at which you ask for canter.

- Progressively wean the horse off the voice and whip aids and on to the classical seat and leg aids.

My advice on the canter depart

- You have to prepare for your canter depart with the greatest care.

- When you are able to obtain a collected walk, straight, light and energetic, your horse will start cantering at the slightest aid. With a well-trained horse, you will be able to ask for canter by 'thinking it'!

- If the horse moves the haunches in and becomes crooked, keep your inside leg on to maintain control of the inside hind leg, which prevents the horse going on two tracks.

- With a straight horse, use the outside leg slightly behind the girth. Do not put your outside leg too far back – the exact position depends on the horse. Before you make the leg aid, take your legs lightly away from the horse's flank.

- Work on your canter departs rigorously. Look for relaxation and perfection. Do not accept any poor or incorrect canter departs. Instead, return to walk, think and start again; this is how you will improve your horse's ride-ability in canter.

With a very young horse who is learning:

- The canter depart is often a source of excitement for a young horse. Do not hesitate to calm your horse at the walk – reassure him, do another exercise and then start again.

- After several strides or a completed circle make a downwards transition after canter, release the reins and reward.

- If your horse starts cantering with too much energy, do not oppose the movement: follow the horse smoothly, stay relaxed and steady him while stroking him. Give the canter aids just before a corner to steady him.

- Keep your demands moderate – don't ask too much, or too often.

HOW TO IMPROVE THE CANTER

Improvement of the canter must be done very progressively. The canter will be improved by executing the canter depart from trot, not by cantering for long periods of time.

Starting from a collected trot on the long side of the arena, try to keep the canter balanced for one or two circles, then make a transition downwards and allow the horse to stretch forwards and downwards into a long rein.

It is then time to work on the canter/walk transition. This has to be done in great relaxation. The transition must be asked for with the upper body, not by the hands. The rider must sit deeper and push forward at the waist. This action will raise the hands, and then all that is necessary is to close the fingers slowly and release to keep the collection. The optimum position is one fist above the withers

Also, work must be done on the collected trot/canter/collected trot transitions and then on canter departs from the walk, above all keeping the horse's movement fluid. These canter departs must be achieved with very small aids.

At the same time, work also on transitions within the canter: collecting and lengthening (see later this chapter). The essential is to proceed softly, with the upper body as the main aid (hands and legs only confirm the aid).

When the horse manages all these exercises, canters in a relaxed way, starts to carry himself and already has a certain degree of collection, it will be time to start with the counter-canter.

Riding the transition from canter to walk. The inside leg supports at the girth. The rider sits deeper and pushes forward at the waist. This action will raise the hands, and then all that is necessary is to close the fingers slowly and release; in this way, the transition to walk is achieved.

My advice on improving the canter

- Always canter on large movements and straight lines with a young horse.
- The young horse must learn to accept the control of the outside rein.
- Try to replace the action of the inside rein with the action of the inside leg.
- Give with your inside rein from time to time, it is the rider's position that asks the horse to 'sit'.
- Act with your seat and legs before you act with your hands.

- The horse should not lean on the reins – he must work in self-carriage. The hands maintain a light contact with the horse's mouth.

- Adapt your aids. Soften the contact with the snaffle bit on the right or left side depending on where the horse is trying to lean on the bit. This can happen if he is seeking balance from the rein when being ridden forwards.

- As soon as your horse is in balance, keep your hands still and maintain a light contact – but support the horse with seat, weight and leg aids.

- Do not put your legs too far back (a lot of riders have this fault).

- Do not 'grip' your legs to the horse's sides – all you will achieve is tension in your body and stiffness in the horse. Allow them to 'drape' around the horse.

- Your legs must be free of tension when you canter, relaxed but ready. They must act in the right place at the right time.

- The inside leg is used to maintain impulsion if the canter becomes 'flat'.

- To sit well and to make yourself taller, put your hips slightly forwards.

- Have a deep seat and your back will be light; your hands will stay light, still and independent.

- Take particular care of the accuracy of your circles when you canter, they must be perfect.

- Always keep enough clearance in the school to be able to make your circle wider.

- Do not let your horse lean to the inside or outside.

- Stay well-seated on your two seat bones.

- Do not exaggerate the bend when you canter: keep your horse on a slight bend, then he will stay relaxed. Do not forget that each horse has a bend that suits him.

- Always keep the same rhythm when you canter, the same energy.

- Before any change of direction or speed, increase the horse's collection.

- Try to have a canter that is identical to the right and to the left, whether you canter or counter-canter (see next section) – same bend, same rhythm, same posture and same collection. This is very important in order to be able to start on the lead changes.

• Never tolerate cross-canter (disunited canter), under saddle or on the lunge.

• Do not let your horse run, do not let him come above or 'through' the bit nor behind the bit and overbent – behind the vertical.

The canter outdoors

Do not hesitate to work on your canter outdoors, on a good flat surface or slightly hilly terrain (Cantering uphill is a good time to practise simple changes, since the gradient will help the horse to 'sit' behind). Be very attentive. Keep your horse on the bit, on the correct bend and in balance.

Watch the speed of the canter and the degree of the horse's relaxation. Make sure your horse stays in balance and in rhythm, and on a soft contact. When the horse stays in good posture, without difficulty, in an active, relaxed canter, it is time to ask for variations in the gait. Riding in a light forward seat relieves the horse and allows the strides to become longer. The rider is in balance on the stirrups, and the hands remain still.

Another common error is to canter too fast and for too long. The horse will put too much weight on the forehand and push the hind legs away behind. Alternate the canter with rising trot to free the horse's back.

Riding up and down hill in a steady, balanced canter in a light seat is of great benefit to improving the canter stride. There again, you must find the right rhythm. On level gound you can canter with a somewhat bigger stride and more energy, but always, I repeat, always, in balance, rounded and with ease.

Lengthening, leading to extension of the canter

While working on the transitions, canter/halt/canter, canter/walk/canter and canter/trot/canter, you will try to shorten and lengthen your horse's canter. The extended canter is the result of impulsion added in the collection. Without needing to be pushed, the horse canters forwards with bigger bounds, sending his forelegs forward from the shoulder, and the back remains supple. The hind leg joints flex and are engaged under the weight of the horse and propel the horse in a forward, upward direction. The size of the strides, the suppleness, the balance and the rhythm define a beautiful 'uphill' and rounded extension in the canter with the poll the highest point.

Preparation and aids for lengthening the canter. The rider prepares by asking for more impulsion whilst the hands remain still, keeping the horse on the bit. When asking for the lengthening, the rider's hands move forward and down, whilst retaining the contact; the rider pushes forward with abdomen, buttocks and back; the legs do very little.

OPPOSITE ABOVE
Extended canter, showing the thrust developed by the hindquarters.

OPPOSITE BELOW
Collected canter – note the engagement of the inside hind leg.

Stiffness, quickening, and imbalance on the shoulders, using strong reins in an effort to gain control, are not good riding but just a battle of strength.

Full extension of the canter is built upon teaching the horse to lengthen progressivly. Here is how to proceed:

- Clearly ask for more collection and a more energetic, forward-thinking canter, on a circle, or on a shoulder-in on the circle, and/or on the short side of the arena.

- Obtain extra impulsion, but without speeding up.

- In the strides preceding the lengthened canter, your hands are very still and keep the horse well on the bit.

- Straighten up and progressively place the horse's shoulders at the beginning of the long side of the arena.

- Carry your contact with the horse's mouth (hand/mouth) forward and down and let your horse lengthen.

- Follow the movement with your abdomen, your seat and your back, together with your leg aids.

- During the lengthened strides, retain the contact with your horse's mouth; maintain a round outline.

- Follow and amplify the lengthened strides with your seat and push very little with your legs, because they sometimes make the horse lose his rhythm.

THE COLLECTED CANTER

This requires:

- A very collected horse, working on shortened bases.

- A perfectly balanced horse, with very active hind legs and haunches, very flexed to allow the raising of the forehand.

- A horse who retains a supple back.

- A neck carried high, with the poll the highest point.

- Forelegs that have to gain in height what they lose in length of step.

- Focused, slower and higher movements from the horse.

- A slow and majestic cadence.

- A superior impulsion with a rigorously straight horse.

- A total absence of stiffness.

- The jaw yields to the slightest action of the rider's fingers.

The school canter, the pinnacle of true collection, is obtained by asking for more and more collection, day after day, by exercising all the joints, by strength-ening the muscles, and developing suppleness.

Circles, lateral work, the transitions canter/halt/rein-back/canter, the shortening and extension of the canter, and the variations of the rhythm are the key exercises to progressively obtaining this majestic gait.

The particular characteristics of the collected canter, especially in its 'school' form are absence of resistance, soft contact, quiet mouth, and light footfalls touching the ground. It requires the willing submission of the horse. The collected canter is the best preparation for leading your horse into the canter pirouette and tempi changes.

COUNTER-CANTER

The horse is ready to start counter-canter when he is consistently relaxed, starts to carry himself and has a certain degree of collection.

The horse counter-canters when, for example, he is on the right rein on a curve to the right, but is bent to the left and canters on the left lead.

When counter-cantering, particularly through a corner or on any arc, the horse has to engage the hind leg to the *inside of the corner/arc* very strongly because it is to the *outside* of his own bend and has to take a larger step. (Note that, in correct parlance, 'inside' and outside' are terms used in reference to the horse not the arena.)

Working the counter-canter enhances the movement of the hindquarters, engages the hind legs and balances the canter. It is therefore a tremendous tool for developing the canter. However, it is a difficult exercise for most young horses and must be ridden with a lot of tact.

It must be introduced starting at the walk. Leave the wall at A or C, half-pass (still walking) to E or B and ask for counter-canter (make sure that your inside shoulder is back – the right shoulder if the canter depart is to the right).

Counter-canter – the horse is leading to the left whilst on the right rein.

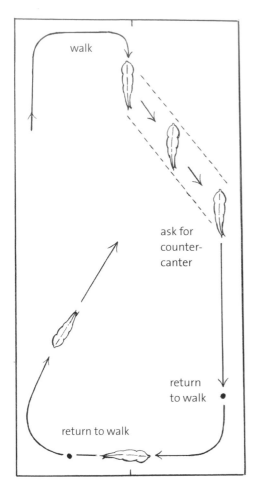

walk

ask for counter-canter

return to walk

return to walk

An exercise for introducing counter-canter via half-pass in walk: turn onto centre line at A or C, half-pass in walk to E or B and ask for counter-canter.

Canter to the end of the long side of the arena and return to walk before the corner. Start again the same way, but pass the first corner in the canter without trying to keep the bend toward the outside (the side of the lead of the canter). Let the horse's spine follow the curve of the circle (corner). This posture is easier on the horse at the beginning.

Return to walk before the second corner. Start again the same way, but then pass the second corner at the canter. Then, take the diagonal so that your horse is back on the true lead and can relax.

Then, start going around the whole arena and on circles in counter-canter.

When the horse is at ease on big circles, progressively reduce the size of the circles. The essential is to keep your horse relaxed and in a good cadence.

My advice on the counter-canter

- When you work on your first circles at the counter-canter, work far away from the wall so you can always enlarge the circle and relieve your horse. Keep a safety margin – if the horse stiffens, enlarge the circle.

- The horse's croup should not escape to the outside.

- Only allow a slight bend to the outside (of the *arena* in this case – see earlier note) when counter-cantering. It is a common error to bend your horse to the inside (of the arena) in a counter-canter. The horse must always have a *slight* bend to the outside of the arena (he may be almost straight, but not bent in an 'S' shape – that is, body bent in one direction, neck in the other!)

- Keep your rhythm, do not let your horse slow down or, even more importantly, do not let him speed up.

- To supple your horse, make sure you work the corners well.

- After a counter-canter circle, when you take the diagonal, keep the acquired collection. Keep your horse well on the aids, on a straight line.

LATERAL EXERCISES IN CANTER

The shoulder-in at canter

This exercise, like all the other lateral exercises, will improve the mobility and the receptivity of your horse.

Start in the corners and on large circles, just asking for a slight bend, then ask on the long side of the arena. You must never force the horse to do it; instead, your seat and your upper torso will encourage him to carry himself during the shoulder-in.

Proceed very progressively; this exercise is very demanding for the engagement of the hind legs, especially on the inside hind. However, it will 'sit the horse down', increase his collection and his submission.

This exercise is tremendously useful for improving the canter.

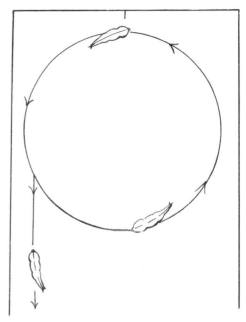

Introducing shoulder-in at canter. On a large circle, ask for slight inside bend then ask for shoulder-in coming off the circle onto a long side of the school.

Half-pass at canter

To ride half-pass in canter, collect more, turn at A or C while keeping a good, balanced canter, and half-pass towards E or B.

When you turn off the wall, make sure you keep your upper body upright and relaxed. Use your legs and seat to push your horse sideways: make sure you keep your shoulders parallel to the horse's shoulders and maintain inside flexion with the reins.

The horse must canter correctly, that means he must jump from one stride to another, not just slide sideways.

Little by little, always with lightness, with the same cadence and keeping the horse 'seated', go through all the exercises related to half-pass: travers (head to the wall), renvers (croup to the wall), circles on both reins with shoulder-in and haunches in (see Chapter 9).

Act progressively; never force the horse – try to feel where the horse is resisting. Executing this work with tact and consideration will allow the development of a very slow canter, while keeping good forward thrust ('impulsion'), cadence and elevation.

At a later stage I will introduce the canter pirouette and even the canter on the spot if the horse is capable.

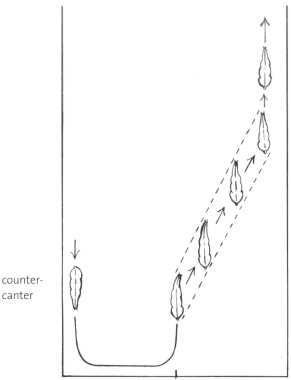

An exercise in half-pass at canter: counter-canter into half-pass.

counter-canter

My advice on the lateral work exercises at canter

- When riding shoulder-in at the canter, do not force the horse to bend to the inside by pulling with the inside rein, but bring the bend inside with your inside leg at the girth, your upper body and by supporting with the outside rein. Both reins lead the forehand to the inside.

- When in half-pass, do not let the horse lean in the direction of the half-pass.

- In a half-pass, the haunches must not escape.

- Pay attention to always keeping the horse's shoulders slightly leading: the shoulders must always precede the haunches.

- If your half-pass starts incorrectly, make a circle in the direction of the half-pass, prepare and start again.

- In half-pass, do not lose the contact with the outside rein; keep the contact during the entire half-pass.

FREQUENTLY ENCOUNTERED PROBLEMS IN CANTER

My horse does not canter

The horse is not ready. Increase the energy of the preceding walk or trot. Ask again but do not harden your aids. Ask yourself whether the co-ordination of your aids is correct.

My horse anticipates the aids

The horse understands what was required, therefore it is a 'goodwill fault' (a good fault).

To begin with, accept the depart then return quietly to walk. Ask again while calming the horse (talk to him) and be very light with your aids before the depart.

My horse takes off when I ask for canter

- Work on the preparation of your canter departs.
- Calm the horse, ride a couple of shoulder-ins.
- Ask for the canter on the other rein.
- Have lighter aids.
- Ride several canter departs with the very lightest of contacts.
- The horse will soon calm down.

My horse raises his neck at the moment of the canter depart

The cause might be in the lack of preparation: the horse is startled. Calm him down, prepare again, and start once more.

Alternatively, it may be that your hand actions are too strong and badly co-ordinated. The hand prevents the movement that was requested with the legs and the action of the inside shoulder. Ask for the canter transition without any hand action; leave the front end alone and quietly release the rein contact.

Whatever the cause of the problem, when you get a correct transition from the horse, reward him. Then use the classical aids again with a lot of tact in your hands.

My horse canters on the wrong lead

The cause lies in the preparation. Your seat and legs tell the horse which leg to canter on. The horse is not then prepared to canter on the correct lead, because of his physical and mental conditioning.

Return to walk and put your horse in a travers position (see Chapter 9), discreetly and delicately. At the moment you straighten the horse, ask for canter. Ask for this canter transition on the wall before a corner.

My horse cross-canters (canters disunited)

The co-ordination of your aids is incorrect. To be correct, your hands and upper torso position the horse to canter on the required lead (for example to the right) and your legs position the haunches to canter on the same lead (the right).

Work harder on the position of your upper torso (the inside shoulder must be a little further back). Ask for canter before a corner.

Very often, the rider's hand blocks the horse's shoulder on one side (too much bend, or inverted bend). Keep an equal contact in both reins.

If none of the errors discussed apply, and everything is prepared well, the cause could be physical problems in the horse – notably in his back, although a hip or a shoulder could be functioning incorrectly.

Feel, observe, think and direct your work on the problem towards the desired result.

My horse cannot differentiate between my leg aid for canter and my leg aid to move the haunches

The outside leg aid to ask for half-pass is really similar to the aid for the canter depart. If the leg acts alone, the horse can get confused. Therefore, you must prepare your request carefully and put your horse in the appropriate balance.

A canter depart is not signalled just by putting the leg behind the girth. Your inside leg must support him. Sit on both seat bones equally with weight into inside stirrup. The forehand must be placed slightly to the inside, away from the wall.

If the horse still puts his haunches in, try asking for canter with your inside leg. Put your shoulders parallel to the horse's shoulders and look straight ahead, in line with the horse's head.

In the early stages of training, you can also use the voice to reinforce the aid. (However, in due course, you must teach the horse to interpret the different aids without being dependent on the voice.)

Finally, when asking for half-pass, put your outside leg further back than you do for canter.

See also '*My horse confuses the outside leg aid for half-pass with the aid for canter*' in the chapter on half-pass.

CHAPTER EIGHT

FLYING CHANGES OF LEAD AT CANTER

PRELIMINARY WORK

Following on from this short section, the rest of the text deals with introducing 'grown up' flying changes to a horse who has reached the appropriate point in his training. However, at a much earlier stage, I believe it is useful to introduce what I call 'baby changes', provided that this is done in the correct way, with due consideration to the horse's physical development and stage of understanding.

I teach these 'baby changes' to a young horse who has just learned to canter correctly, introducing it as fun, using my clear aids so that the youngster follows my weight on a new change of direction. Although these early changes will be rather fast and feel unbalanced, the rider must remain in complete balance, giving the youngster confidence. A youngster will naturally change from left to right or right to left when cantering in the field and changing direction; all we are doing here is the same, but letting him know he is also able to do this with a rider. Reward whenever a change is accomplished, never losing patience or being over-zealous with the aids, I would then forget about the changes until his other work is consolidated.

(In a similar vein, with a view to the flying changes, when first teaching the counter-canter, if your horse changes lead, do not reprimand him; remain calm and ask him again for the counter-canter keeping your aids precise. You need him to be proud that he can change, and your tolerance will assist when it comes to asking for the flying change.)

ABOVE AND OPPOSITE BELOW
An exuberant single change from left to right canter,
showing clearly the sequence of change of legs.

THE SINGLE FLYING CHANGE OF LEAD

The horse canters on either the left or right lead. During a flying change of
lead, the horse switches canter lead during the time of suspension. For
example, the horse changes from a right-lead canter to a left-lead canter while
staying on the same line. 'The flying change of lead is a fresh canter depart
inside the canter' – Nuno Oliveira.

    This is an easy exercise when the horse is calm and straight, and has a
good-quality canter. However, with very reactive and complicated horses, introducing the flying change of lead can be very difficult and time-consuming,
and will require a lot of work and experience on the rider's part.

The aids

The description is for a flying change from the right to the left lead. Confirm the aids of the right-lead canter:

- The horse is straight, calm and balanced.

- The rider's right leg is at the girth, relaxed.

- The rider's left leg is slightly behind the girth.

- The rider's shoulder are always parallel to the horse's shoulders.

- Sit equally on both seat bones.

- The contact with the new outside rein is slightly stronger.

To change lead, simultaneously invert all the aids:

- The new outside leg touches the horse lightly behind the girth.

- The left leg goes just in front of the girth.

- The horse must remain straight (hardly any flexion left).

- The contact with the right (outside) rein is slightly stronger.

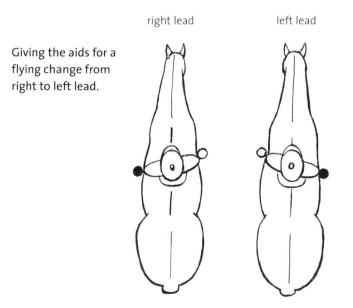

right lead   left lead

Giving the aids for a flying change from right to left lead.

My advice about the aids

The important thing is to physically and mentally prepare the horse for the flying change of lead. Get a rounded and relaxed canter (rider also relaxed) before changing lead. Feel the canter accurately, find the right cadence for the horse, and act at exactly the right moment.

The change itself – the inversion of the aids – has to be done with a minimum amount of physical movement or pressure. Your aids have to be precise, *fast* and light. Keep your legs very relaxed. Use the fat part of your calf as much as possible and the spur if needed. The spur touches delicately but with precision. Move your new outside leg back slightly just before touching the horse.

During the flying change, do not shift your seat forward and fold at the waist. Above all, do not look down to see if the lead change worked. Look toward the horse's ears.

Be very calm and do not get heavy with the aids; always keep your horse calm and relaxed.

Do not let your horse speed up and do not lose the contact during the lead change. Keep the same tempo on the same line; keep the horse straight – do nothing to provoke crookedness.

Aim to ride only a few flying changes, but always of good quality. After several flying changes, ride very calmly to the same spot again, release the contact momentarily by giving and retaking the reins and do not ask for a flying change this time.

When can one ask for the first flying change of lead?

The horse must have attained the following qualities:

- He must be relaxed in shoulder-in and half-pass at walk and trot.

- He must be engaged on the bit, know how to halt squarely and rein-back. He must be able to go from canter to walk and walk to canter.

- He must be calm at the canter, balanced, straight, light and have a certain roundness and a good canter cadence.

- He must be able to counter-canter in any circumstance.

- He must have a very good, serene canter depart, on either lead, any time, from the walk or the halt.

Such a horse is ready to give his first flying change of lead.

Teaching the first flying change of lead

1. The first method is from true canter to true canter (in this example, from the right to the left lead:

   - First, during the session, seek a well-balanced, relaxed and rounded canter and counter-canter on both reins.

   - Ride several canter and counter-canter departs from the walk on both reins.

   - Ride transitions between canter and walk.

   Ride several transitions from canter to walk and from walk to canter. There are many variations on where you can ask for a flying change. Do not always ride the same exercise. The horse can become a little tense and lose concentration.

   One example is as follows:

   - On the right rein, ride an active and shortened collected canter on the short side. Ride a 10 metre circle at M, and when you are coming out of the circle, ride a very short diagonal line towards C. Keep the horse straight and in the same tempo. Sit quietly and change your leg position to left canter as you approach C. The new outside leg acts lightly behind the girth, and the new inside leg is taken slightly forwards, but is not actively used. The tempo is controlled with the new outside rein. The whip can be tactfully used to help reinforce the aids to change.

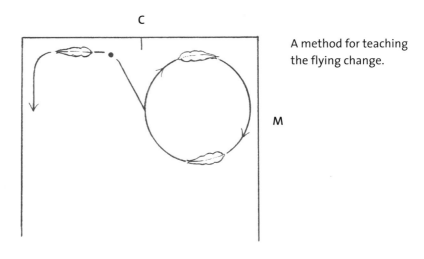

A method for teaching the flying change.

- The horse should make his first flying change – so praise him!

- The change occurs as the horse reaches the track – he should go around the corner between C and H in left canter.

- Repeat this exercise two or three times in the same place, and on both reins.

Once you have mastered this exercise, try riding it in other places around the arena. If the horse comes off your aids, make no further changes, but ride the same exercises just in a steady canter. The horse must learn to wait. We must always keep the horse under control.

- A further exercise is to canter on the inside track and ask for the flying change. All exercises must be ridden like a game and be fun for the horse – not forced!

2. Another way to proceed is from true canter to counter-canter, in this example, changing from the left lead:

- Canter to the left and make two circles.

- Join the wall and at the beginning of the long side of the arena, ask for a flying lead change in the following way:

  – Just before the long side of the arena, at the completion of your circle, bring your horse's head to the left with a subtle action of your left rein (slightly higher and slightly inward).

  – Change lead with an action of the left rein, moving your right shoulder back, followed instantaneously by an action of the whip on the left haunch and the action of the left leg behind the girth (whip and leg act together).

  – Note that, in this case, you use lateral aids.

  – The action of the left rein tends to 'close' the left side and 'open' the right side.

  – The horse changes lead.

3. Another way to proceed, used by some trainers, is from true canter to counter-canter through a trot transition. This method is explained in detail

under Frequently Encountered Problems later this chapter (see *The horse 'explodes' when changing lead*).

My advice about teaching the flying change

The old riding masters began flying changes when the horse was strong enough. The change of leg occurs in the moment of suspension when the horse springs sufficiently off the ground and in balance. This is only possible when the horse is strong in his haunches.

Changes are easy to ride, provided the horse is in balance and makes even, balanced strides.

Learning flying changes should follow these basic rules:

- Never be impatient or anxious about the exercise.

- Do not make the exercise too difficult – if the horse does not understand, take a step back in the horse's training and reinforce simpler movements.

- Do not allow the haunches to be in during the preparatory canter.

- Your aids must be fast and in time with the horse's canter stride, but never hard or heavy – use tact and psychology.

- Do not ask too much, and, above all, reward and relax your horse once he understands.

- In the beginning, when the horse is learning, you can emphasize the movement of your upper body slightly to amplify the movement of the horse.

- The first couple of sessions, always ask for the lead change at the same spot, choosing the most physically and mentally propitious spot for your horse.

- After single flying changes, always go back to the same spot and canter through calmly, without changing lead.

- When your flying changes are confirmed, change lead or canter through the area without changing lead, in turn.

- With a more difficult horse that always changes with its hindquarters raised, choose the second method described to introduce the change.

- Do not let the horse's shoulders 'stick to the wall' during the flying changes. Stay a little off the wall.

FREQUENTLY ENCOUNTERED PROBLEMS IN THE SINGLE CHANGE

The horse does not change lead

- The horse might not be ready for flying changes – see *When can one ask for the first flying change of lead?*

- The canter might not be well-enough prepared, it must be balanced, energetic and relaxed.

- The aids might not be in tune with the horse's movement (applied at the right time) or they may lack precision.

The horse changes lead, but incorrectly or imprecisely

- The horse only changes lead in front. The hand action precedes the leg action; the leg action is not precise enough and is not applied at the right time. If, despite the rider attending to the aids, the horse persists on changing in front only, it may be necessary to use a touch of the whip on the haunch on the same side as the rider's leg.

- The horse changes lead over two strides. The rider's aids are not simultaneous; they are badly co-ordinated. Alternatively, the horse is not straight in the shoulders or in the haunches.

- The horse changes lead before being asked. This is because the horse understands the exercise and anticipates the aids. Calm him, reassure him and start again with well-confirmed aids for the canter depart. If the horse persists in anticipating, pass the same spot a few times without changing lead. Perhaps also pick another spot to change lead.

- The horse changes lead late. This can occur because of lack of preparation in the preceding canter, because the horse was not ready at the time of asking, or because of lack of decisiveness and precision in the aids. (Precision is everything!)

The horse speeds up after the change of lead

Use lighter, quieter aids. Calm the horse by reassuring him with your voice, come out of canter after a couple of strides and walk on long reins. Start again with great calmness.

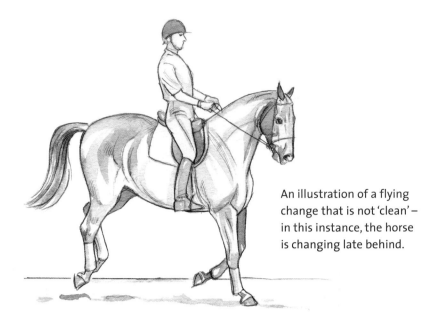

An illustration of a flying change that is not 'clean' – in this instance, the horse is changing late behind.

The horse steps sideways and rocks heavily

The change of bend is too great (keep your reins practically equal) and/or the leg acts too far back or too strongly. Other aids may also be too strong.

The horse 'explodes' when changing lead

- The horse might not be mentally ready for a flying change of lead. Resume training to reach the required conditions (see: When can one ask for the first flying change of lead?)

- Your aids might be too fast or too strong (in general, the action of the leg and upper body). Act with more tact and softness. Reassure and calm the horse before and after the change.

- The horse is too reactive, sometimes feverish in his behaviour. Some highly strung, very reactive horses resist and 'explode' when they first learn the changes of lead. However, the lead change cannot be deconstructed. It must be prepared over a long time of course; but you end up having to ask for the entire change of lead all at once.

  With this kind of horse, it is better to use the following method to teach lead changes (example is from the right to the left):

  – Work on canter departs from the trot on both reins and on both leads.

  – Obtain a rounded, calm, relaxed but energetic canter.

– Take a diagonal at right-lead canter and ride a transition to trot at the end of the first third of the diagonal. Do this several times.

– Then, after the trot, canter to the left at the end of the second third of the diagonal. Join the wall and follow with a circle to the left. Reward.

– Little by little, reduce (with great calmness) the number of strides of trot between the right-lead and left-lead canter.

– Finally, smoothly slow down your right-lead canter to prepare for a transition, but instead of going into trot, tactfully switch your canter aids. The horse will change lead.

When teaching a 'sharp' horse at the beginning, it is more about *authorizing* the lead change (so that the horse understands what is going on) than about asking for a lead change.

My horse inserts a stride of trot

This problem relates to a query from a pupil who elaborated by saying: 'My horse changes lead easily from the right to the left, but systematically adds a stride of trot in the changes from the left to the right. At the first attempt, he gives me a correct change and then falls back into his old habit by anticipating my demand and inserts a stride of trot before changing lead.'

This is an interesting problem, and not easy to resolve. Two questions that occurred to me initially were:

• Is your horse related to Trotters? (Down the years, horses from trotting stock have sometimes posed problems in canter work.)

• When teaching your first changes of lead, did you ask directly for a flying change or did you change through trot?

By way of resolution, I think the strides preceding the lead change must be carefully ridden: collect more, confirm the left canter aids while staying light, have well-timed, fast, clear and precise aids to change to the right. To analyse further:

1. Try to modify your way of proceeding, to feel the very moment you must act by anticipating or delaying the aids, by acting faster or more smoothly,

by having a clearer action of the upper body and by softening or closing your fingers more.

2. Try to determine whether one spot works better than another (straight line, diagonal, before or after the corner…). Figure out if it is easier to change from counter-canter to true canter or vice versa.

3. See if it is better to lead into a change in the same, increased or decreased cadence. Find out which are the most favourable stride length and energy.

4. Look for the posture or balance (more or less on the bit, more or less collected, haunches lowered more or less, neck lower or higher, horse more or less free…) that are most favourable to your horse, in which he performs best.

Addressing these points should put you on the right track. Watch… observe… All these factors have great influence on your horse's psyche. It is by modifying the elements that you will obtain the desired result. *Very little is often enough…* !

TEMPI CHANGES

Tempi changes are series of flying changes made every prescribed number of strides.

When can we start to work on tempi changes?

The following is a list of what the horse must already be able to do in order to begin:

- He must be able to execute calm and relaxed single flying changes of lead on the long side of the arena or on the diagonal, on both reins, from canter to counter-canter, or counter-canter to canter.

- If possible, the horse should also be able to do single changes on the short side of the arena and on a large circle.

- He must stay perfectly straight during a single change.

- He must keep the same rhythm and the same degree of collection (not losing the posture) during the change.

If these criteria are in place, the horse is ready to work on tempi changes, up to changes every two strides.

Teaching the horse tempi changes up to every two strides

I would start with two single changes, one at the beginning and one at the end of the long side of the arena. Make one or two left-rein circles to prepare, with your horse nicely cadenced, relaxed, rounded and very straight.

Change your lead to the right at the precise moment you reach the long side of the arena, by moving your right shoulder and your left leg back (inversion of aids).

Keep the horse straight. Keep the horse in a rounded outline, nicely calm, nicely straight, on the long side of the arena, confirming the right-lead canter at every stride.

Ask for the second change of lead just before the corner. Keep the rhythm: reward – walking on a long rein.

Proceed in the same way for the following days on the two long sides of the arena and on both reins on the inside track. Then, change lead at the end of the first third and at the end of the second third of the long side of the arena (still two changes, but closer together).

Ask first from canter and then from counter-canter. Next, ride the same exercise on the diagonals.

Then, ask for maybe four changes: two on the first long side of the arena and two on the other side. You can then start reducing the number of strides between changes. With tact, moderation and concentration, ask for tempi changes every four strides. Proceed with the same technique as before, but increase collection and above all, keep the horse calm, cadenced and straight.

Work on the tempi changes every four strides for two or three weeks until they are well confirmed. When the horse gives the change every four strides, easily and calmly and without anticipating the aids, you can start asking for changes every three strides and then every two strides. Most important of all, stay calm, straight and cadenced and maintain a secure and quiet seat.

My advice on tempi changes

My fundamental advice on teaching the horse tempi changes up to every two strides is the same as for the single flying changes of lead. Never be in a hurry; take your time. This may take several weeks.

Alternate your schooling sessions – some with flying changes and some without flying changes.

Your major concern will be to continuously improve the quality of your canter. You must obtain the same quality of canter on both reins (same cadence, same degree of collection, same straightness).

'Ask little, ask often, reward a lot' should be your philosophy.

Count the number of strides between flying changes in your head in order to anticipate. You must always know where you are and what you are going to do. Between the changes, apply your canter aids with tact, always at the right moment. Keep your inside shoulder slightly back, and keep contact with your outside rein to control collection. Also:

- Do not harden your aids.

- Do not, at this stage, make lateral movements of your body to let (or make) the horse change.

- Do not look at the horse's forelegs, and do not let his ears out of sight.

Frequently encountered problems with tempi changes

The problems encountered with tempi changes are essentially the same as those encountered with the single changes. However, as you reduce the number of strides between changes, specific problems might appear.

The horse moves sideways during the changes

- Do not put your outside leg too far back, use mostly the top of your calf, and higher.

- Take a bit more contact on the new outside rein.

- Be subtle with your upper body.

The horse loses cadence

- Be aware that there is a specific degree of collection and cadence to the different tempi changes (four, three and two strides). The smaller the number of strides allowed between changes, the greater the collection must be.

- Very often, the rider's hands are used too much: the horse slows down, or he lifts his head or twists himself, and then accelerates.

One side is stiffer than the other (one leg is used with more strength than the other)

- The aids may be too strong (or not clear enough) on one side.

- The horse perhaps twists to one side and needs time to put himself straight again – keep your horse straight.

- The horse may tend to 'lean' on the wall of the arena – move slightly away from the wall.

Note that the canter must be equal on both reins before starting with the one-time changes.

The horse anticipates the next change

- Confirm the aids (for the canter) between each change of lead to stay on the chosen lead.

- Work calmly in walk for a while, before beginning again.

- Keep your legs very relaxed, do not clamp them against the horse's sides.

ONE-TIME CHANGES

In the one-time changes, the horse changes lead every stride, for a set number of strides. To be ready to learn the one-time changes, the horse must successfully execute all the preceding exercises; he must be able to change lead easily every two strides, without the slightest sign of nervousness. See the sequences of photos on the following pages.

Teaching one-time changes

- First, increase the energy of the canter. Obtain a very good cadence, a nice impulsion in your canter, just a little faster than for two-time changes.

- The horse must be absolutely straight.

- At the end of the long side of the arena, cantering on the true (correct lead), change to the counter-canter and then immediately back to the correct lead.

- Repeat two or three times, reward and put the horse back in his stable.

PAGES 148–151 ▶
A sequence of one-time changes, beginning in right lead. By the fourth picture, the horse has changed to left lead; four pictures further on, he is in right lead and, by the final picture, he has switched again to left lead.

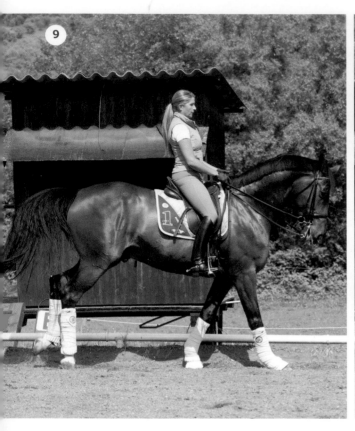

ABOVE AND OPPOSITE
ABOVE
Sequence of one-time
changes continued
from previous two
pages.

Work on this over the following days.

Next, obtain the same sequence in the middle of the long side of the arena, at the first third, the second third…

To obtain three one-time changes in a row, counter-canter and at the middle of long side of the arena, canter/counter-canter/canter, keeping your aids light.

Continue working on the three one-time changes in a row until these are mastered and then go to four in a row. Increase the amount progressively, once the previous number have been obtained successfully.

My advice on teaching one-time changes

- Do not move your upper torso overtly, and stay in a good posture. (In the next section, under *The horse loses cadence*, I have explained that changing lead every stride produces a kind of barely perceptible swinging of the upper torso; this is a natural response, not a deliberate action on the rider's part.)

- Do not ever look at the ground because you will lose the right rhythm: look ahead, between your horse's ears.

- Your hands must have a good contact with the horse's mouth, and the horse's head must stay straight.

- Use your legs more to signal the changes, but do not move your leg back much – if you do, you will lose too much time and miss the next change.

- Touch with your new outside leg immediately after the first change… TAC/ TAC/ TAC…. and above all do not clamp your legs on to the horse – they must stay relaxed so that they can give the aid to change quietly.

Frequently encountered problems with one-time changes

The same problems are encountered as in single changes and tempi changes up to every two strides.

The horse loses cadence

- The cadence of your canter is not the right one.

- The canter is not collected enough and not energetic enough and on the forehand.

- The rhythm and timing of your actions are wrong. Changing lead every stride produces a kind of barely perceptible swinging of the upper torso, which demands excellent co-ordination of the aids and great relaxation. Try to have a better perception of your body, a mental picture of it (body awareness).

Good posture and timing are essentials for riding one-time changes, which are repetitions of the patterns shown here.

The horse alternates between one-time and two-time changes

Remember that tempi changes at every stride are very difficult for the rider, whose actions must be executed with great speed and precision while the legs remain relaxed. If the horse loses the cadence and collection of the canter required for one-time changes, he will change maybe every two strides. To avoid or remedy this:

- Concentrate on your legs and keep a light contact with both reins.

- Have the rhythm of the changes in your head and in your body.

- Stay well aligned, do not slow down, do not speed up, and watch out that you rigorously keep the same balance and the same tempo.

The horse does not manage the third one-time change

It is relatively easy to obtain the left/right or right/left changes, but typically there is difficulty in obtaining the third change in a row: the third change must be super-fast, but above all more refined than the two preceding ones. Therefore, there is a tendency to exaggerate it too much, or to ask too hard. Try to be aware of this and avoid these errors. If the horse needs firmer aids on one side, he will tend to change more easily on this side. Fine adjustment is the best way. Flying change must flow and be ridden forwards.

CHAPTER NINE

THE LATERAL EXERCISES

The lateral exercises – in particular, shoulder-in – play an important part in the training of the horse, improving suppleness, straightness, strength, attentiveness to the aids and helping to progress the horse towards a capacity for true collection. To aid the learning process, they should be introduced initially to the horse in the order in which they appear in this chapter.

THE TURN ON THE FOREHAND

The turn on the forehand, carried out equally on both reins, is an exercise to teach the horse the first lessons in moving away from the leg. It thus serves a similar purpose to leg-yielding (see next section). The exercise can be taught from the ground (in-hand work) as well as from the saddle.

Turn on the forehand mounted is also a valuable exercise to help the rider to learn co-ordination of seat, leg and rein.

However, it is not an exercise that should be used too often, as it does not encourage the forward movement of the horse. Indeed, because the horse is restricted to moving forward only minimally, it can have quite a discouraging effect on a young or green horse if overdone. For the same reasons it is not advisable to conduct a complete 180° turn every time; instead, most turns should be of 90° only, and the horse should be sent forward immediately on completion of the turn. If a green horse shows signs of having been upset by turn on the forehand, it would thus be better for him to continue with varied leg-yield exercises.

Aside from teaching response to the sideways-nudging leg, the turn on the forehand exercise assists us in placing the inner hind leg closer to the horse's mid-line, thus putting it closer to the body and more in front of the other hind leg. In doing this, the horse's hip and stifle joints are being exercised, which enhances both their flexibility and their strength.

Riding a turn on the forehand

We begin developing this exercise by halting the horse squarely on the inside track (three-quarter line). We then start to turn the horse with his head facing towards the outside track. (Turns of just 90° can be performed by halting the horse at right angles to the outside track, with his head quite near the wall. However, if he is to describe a 180° turn, there must be sufficient room for him to complete the turn without banging his hindquarters against the wall.)

The rider asks for a turn on the forehand by halting squarely and, calmly, but without delay, indicating the direction of the turn with the inside rein, whilst maintaining the contact of the outside rein to prevent the horse covering too much ground. See sequence of photos beginning on page 158.

Turns on the forehand of just 90° degrees can be performed at right angles to the outside track, with the horse's head quite near the wall. However, if he is to describe a 180° turn, there must be sufficient room for him to complete the turn without banging his hindquarters against the wall.

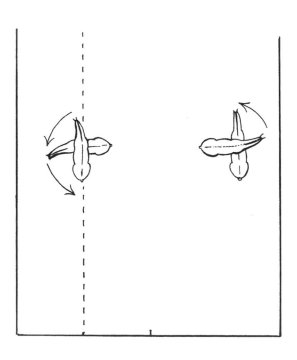

The inside leg should be positioned just behind the girth and is used to nudge the quarters over step-by-step.

The outside leg is also placed behind the girth for the purpose of receiving and controlling each of the horse's steps.

Example

- For a turn on the forehand to the right, halt the horse square off the track or across the centre line.

- Using your right leg and right rein will indicate to the horse the direction of the turn (to the right, in this example).

- Your left leg and rein will support the outside frame of the horse and control the speed.

- As you use your right leg the haunches will move over to the left; your left leg will receive and control the movement. The hind legs will cross as the forehand continues to make a semi-circle to the right.

- Once the desired turn is completed, the horse is ridden forward immediately into walk.

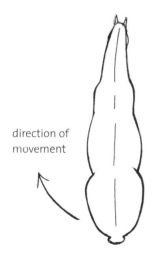

direction of movement

Turn on the forehand: the hindquarters turn around the forehand; the inside hind leg steps across the outside hind.

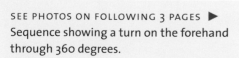

SEE PHOTOS ON FOLLOWING 3 PAGES ▶
Sequence showing a turn on the forehand through 360 degrees.

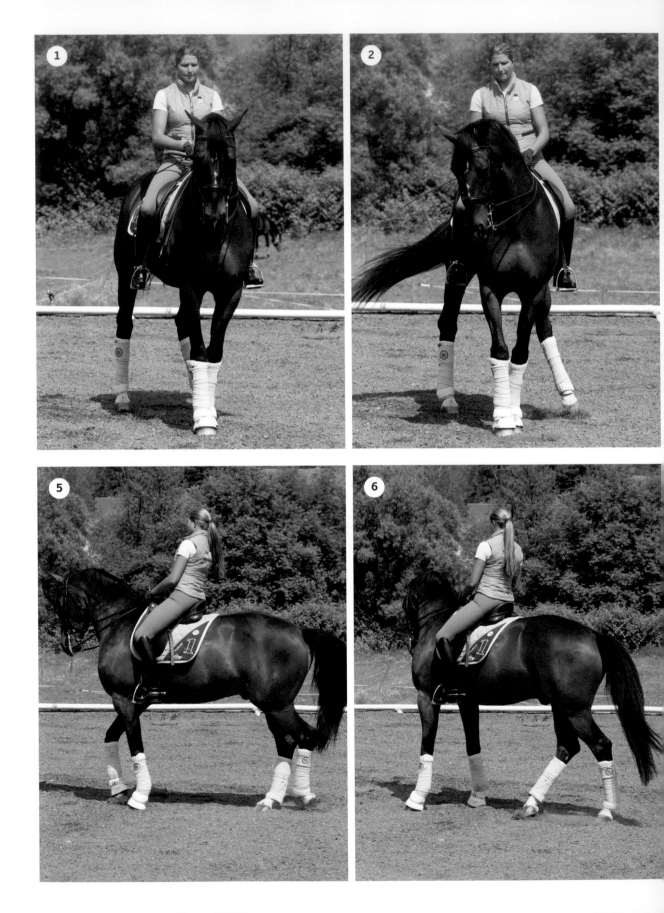

Points for attention

- The movement must be performed in the correct sequence of walk steps.

- A slight bend in the direction of the turn must be maintained at all times.

- No backwards stepping or hurrying must occur at any stage.

- The horse must continue to accept the contact without resistance in the mouth or dropping of the bit.

Faults and corrections

- The horse may show too much neck bend in the direction in which he is going. Counteract or correct this by using less inside rein and more inside leg into the outside rein. The contact remains light but at no point are both reins pulled backwards.

- Resistance to or not accepting the bit can be corrected by maintaining (or adjusting) the outside rein contact.

- Any tendency for the horse to step backwards can be counteracted by the rider maintaining a 'forward' impulse by keeping both legs in contact with the horse.

- The horse walking in a small circle occurs mainly because of lack of co-ordination of the aids. To correct this it is first necessary to establish a square halt. Following this, at first ask for only one step, which must be followed by immediate reward upon response. (However, with a very front-heavy horse it may be necessary to allow a very small circle to assist sufficient lifting of the forelegs – see below).

- Loss of the correct sequence of footfalls usually occurs as a consequence of the horse lacking a 'forward' impulse.

One major issue that can be encountered when riding turns on the forehand is that the horse might fail to lift his forefeet sufficiently (in particular if the horse is front-heavy). Normally, should this be the case, the horse's legs get more or less twisted around one another in such a way, that any further movement becomes virtually impossible for him. Another result of a horse's front-heaviness is that only one (usually the outer) foreleg is not being lifted

A potential problem with the turn on the forehand can arise with horses who are naturally 'front-heavy'/on the forehand. The lifting of the hind legs tends to move the centre of gravity forward, further loading the forelimbs, which can lead to loss of co-ordination.

sufficiently. In such an instance, the horse would regain balance by stepping around on the inner foot. In order to avoid these faults we must ensure that the horse's front end is describing a very small-scale circle as opposed to staying in one place throughout the movement.

LEG-YIELDING

This movement can be ridden in walk and trot and also in canter. We start teaching the young horse this exercise as an early introduction to lateral work and a simple understanding of the aids used. Collection is not required.

The leg-yield is a forward-sideways movement with the horse moving on two tracks. The horse's body is straight with a slight flexion at the poll, the flexion being opposite to the direction in which the horse is moving.

The aids

The leg-yield can be from a circle, a diagonal line or along the track.

When leg-yielding to the right, the rider picks a diagonal line that the horse's forefeet follow: the rider's inside leg (left) sits behind the girth, pushing the horse over: the outside leg (right) keeps supporting the horse so as to keep the movement forward and on a consistent line. The inside hand (left) indicates the bend, and the outside hand (right) leads the way, controlling the straightness and the speed of the forward movement. For leg-yielding to the left, the aids are reversed.

Common faults and corrections

- Loss of impulsion and rhythm, failing to move forward. As with all lateral work, the 'forward' element must take precedence over the 'sideways' element. Bearing this in mind will help correct co-ordination of the aids.

- Straightness (consistency of flexion and line of travel) lost because quarters are leading or trailing. The rider must ensure that the outside rein is supporting the outside shoulder and that the inside leg asks the horse to work into the outside rein sufficiently.

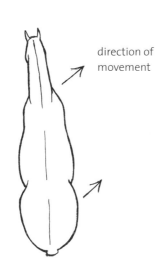

direction of movement

Aids for leg-yield.

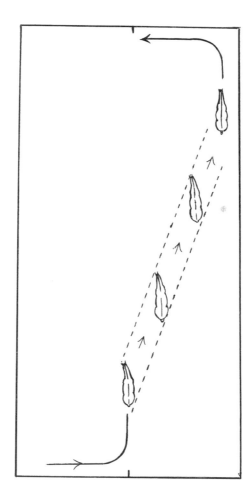

The principles of leg-yielding.

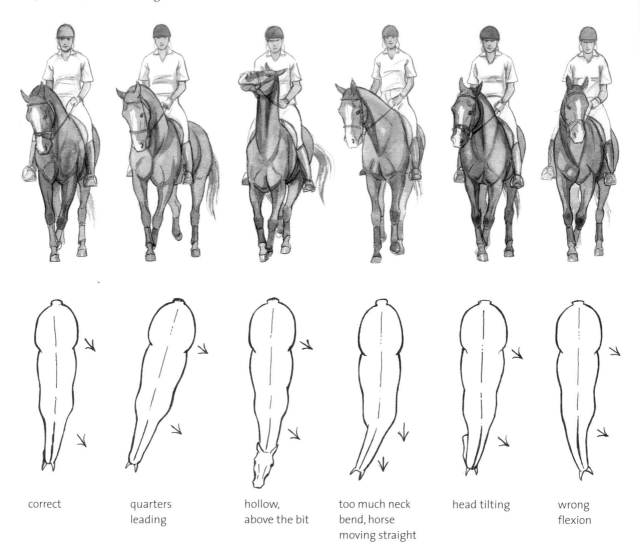

| correct | quarters leading | hollow, above the bit | too much neck bend, horse moving straight | head tilting | wrong flexion |

Leg-yielding: correct method and common errors.

- Too much neck bend or tilting at the poll. The horse's ears must be level and the rider looking forwards between the horse's ears. There must be enough support from the outside rein and the horse must be asked to go more forwards on the chosen line to the contact.

- Failing to cross over behind. The rider must be supple in the back to allow the movement of the horse's back muscles as the legs cross. The horse must work into the outside rein. The inside leg asks the horse to go more sideways. Rising trot can help when riding lateral work.

SHOULDER-IN

History and background

The French riding master and trainer François de la Guérinière is usually credited with inventing the shoulder-in during the eighteenth century. This was because he adapted the movement for use on straight lines. However, his compatriot Antoine de Pluvinel used the basic shoulder-in and many other lateral movements more than a century earlier. De Pluvinel used the exercise especially around a pillar to increase the horse's suppleness and to get him used to the aids, especially the leg aids. Other early trainers who experimented with exercises broadly similar to shoulder-in were the sixteenth-century French trainer Salomon de la Broue and the English aristocrat of the seventeenth century, the Duke of Newcastle.

Since de la Guérinière's time, the shoulder-in has been widely accepted to be the most important suppling, strengthening and preparatory exercise that exists for the rider training a horse.

Description

Shoulder-in is a lateral movement in which the horse is bent slightly but uniformly from head to tail around the inside leg of the rider. The shoulders and forelegs are brought off the straight line, the inside foreleg passing in front of the outside foreleg. The hind legs remain on the track, and continue to proceed straight forward. Thus the horse's body forms an angle to the straight line and he travels partially sideways and can be ridden on 3 or 4 tracks.

The angle to the straight line should not normally exceed 30°. The usual angle (and that required in dressage tests) is such that the horse moves on three tracks:

1st track – the outside hind.

2nd track – the inside hind and outside fore on the same track.

3rd track – the inside fore.

However, if required, as a training exercise, the angle may be increased until the horse is travelling on four tracks, with each foot making its own track.

Especially in competition dressage, shoulder-in is usually performed on three tracks (left-hand picture), but it can also be performed on four tracks (right-hand picture).

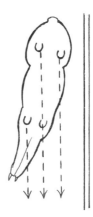 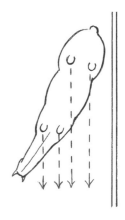

Shoulder-in on three tracks.

Shoulder-in is of great value when carried out correctly; it is a suppling exercise which also helps to increase collection. The horse is encouraged to bend his body round in front of the inside hind leg so that this hind leg does more than its usual amount of work and is the prime driving limb for propulsion. You are 'loading' the inside hind leg. It also teaches the rider to control the horse's shoulders.

It can be ridden in walk, trot and canter, but the main schooling value is derived when it is ridden in a correctly shortened trot. In this respect, the horse is ready to begin the exercise when he is able to shorten his trot steps while maintaining rhythm, impulsion, relaxation and suppleness. The quality of the shoulder-in will depend on the quality of the shortened trot preceding it.

Shoulder-in on four tracks.

With respect to his understanding of the lateral aids, the horse must be bending and flexing correctly through corners and circles, able to leg-yield and have learned to take and accept the outside rein, giving with his jaw without slowing down.

The aids

Shoulder-in may be ridden down the long side, down the centre line, or on a circle. (Shoulder-in on a circle is a good way to introduce the movement. The positioning aids –right bend or left bend depending whether the circle is to the left or to the right – are already in place, so the rider asks for the shoulder-in by increasing the aid with the inside leg and outside rein, turning the upper body slightly inwards on the circle.)

Prepare for shoulder-in by shortening the trot steps (sitting trot) and possibly making a 10-metre circle in the corner at the beginning of the long side to encourage the correct bend. (It's more difficult to establish the lateral bend on a straight line, especially if your horse is not used to the movement.)

Although the main schooling benefit of shoulder-in is derived from riding the exercise in a correctly shortened trot, it can also be ridden in walk and, as shown here, in canter.

Then proceed down the long side, bringing the forehand off the track as though beginning a second circle. At the moment when the shoulders and forelegs leave the track, the outside hand prevents the horse from gaining ground, and controls the degree of bend to the inside. The inside leg, on the girth, maintains the impulsion and encourages the forward and sideways movement, while the outside leg is a little behind the girth and prevents the quarters moving out. Essentially, you are pushing the horse along the track from your inside leg into the outside rein.

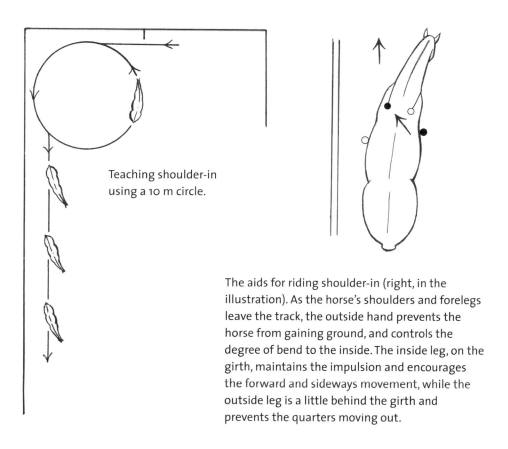

Teaching shoulder-in using a 10 m circle.

The aids for riding shoulder-in (right, in the illustration). As the horse's shoulders and forelegs leave the track, the outside hand prevents the horse from gaining ground, and controls the degree of bend to the inside. The inside leg, on the girth, maintains the impulsion and encourages the forward and sideways movement, while the outside leg is a little behind the girth and prevents the quarters moving out.

It is important to sit centrally in the saddle and look between the horse's ears. You will be able to see where you are going by looking up the track out of the corners of your eyes. Make sure your shoulders are parallel to your horse's shoulders.(I prefer to bring my inside shoulder back rather than move my outside shoulder forward.) If your head and shoulders are not in line with the horse's head and shoulders, you may unbalance the horse and spoil the movement.

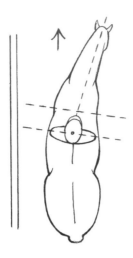

The rider's position for shoulder-in.

- The rider's shoulders should be at the same angle as the horse's shoulders.
- The rider should look between the horse's ears.

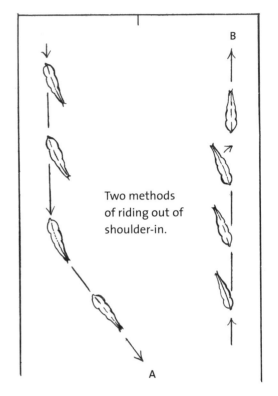

Two methods of riding out of shoulder-in.

A – curving across the school

B – bringing the horse's back to the track

On completion of the shoulder-in, you may either ride forward on a curve across the school or straighten the horse by bringing his shoulders back on to the straight line. The former is less demanding and also more encouraging and rewarding to a young horse. The latter is used in competitions and is a greater test of obedience. If you do intend to straighten the shoulder-in, do so before the next corner, not at the corner.

Checklist of important points

- *Do not try to hold the horse in position with the inside rein* – it just will not work. Be as soft as you can with your inside rein.

- Sit at the correct angle – your shoulders at the same angle as your horse's (parallel to them) and your head straight (not looking to the right or left). If the horse's ears are in front of you, you must have the correct angle. I use the horse's ears as one would use gun sights.

- Stay supple. The horse needs your body to be totally neutral and 'giving' while he is co-ordinating his body to perform the movement. If he has to cope with your stiffness, it will make the exercise harder for him.

- Once you have the shoulder-in posture and it's working, do not keep asking for shoulder-in. Simply adjust the movement (if necessary). If you keep asking for the movement as you did at its inception, your horse will become confused and try to do something else to avoid the annoying repetition of the same aid. If he is doing what you wish, just let him do it.

Common faults and corrections

- The horse may lose impulsion and thus will not continue to accept the bit. To avoid this, always give precedence to the 'forward' element of lateral work.

- The angle of the shoulder-in may vary. The variation should be corrected by the rider making the aids consistent and finding a balance between leg and hand. (This problem sometimes starts when a rider asks for too great an angle at the beginning of the movement.)

- The horse may bend his neck too much, putting excessive weight on his outside shoulder. This is usually caused by insufficient outside rein contact or too much inside rein contact.

- The horse's quarters sometimes go out instead of the shoulders coming in: it is necessary to pay particular attention to bringing the shoulders in at the beginning of the movement and controlling the swing of the quarters with the outside leg.

- Varying rhythm and differing angles on left and right reins are problems which may be related to a degree of one-sidedness. These must be felt and corrected.

- The value of the exercise is lost if the horse becomes tense and is no longer relaxed and supple in his movement.

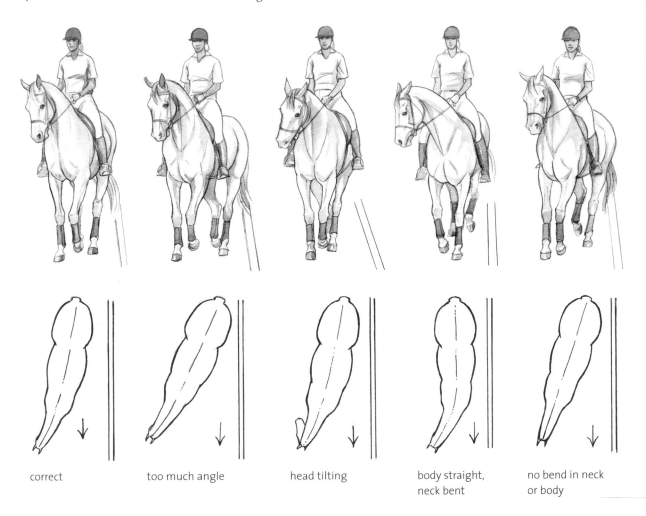

| correct | too much angle | head tilting | body straight, neck bent | no bend in neck or body |

Shoulder-in on three tracks: correct method and common errors.

How to correct the angle

When first starting the shoulder-in, the horse will find the extra work difficult and exacting: he will initially be reluctant to give you a true angle in shoulder-in. He will try to avoid the work by keeping his body straight, parallel to the wall or track, and just bending his head and neck. (This is also a problem if the rider is using too much inside rein!) This posture is a travesty of the correct movement and looks ugly.

If your horse is going forward, whether in walk or trot, and you are absolutely certain that you are not pulling on the inside rein, but he is just not bending through his body, you will have to correct the angle sooner rather than later. To get the correct bend, proceed as follows:

- Momentarily take the inside rein in a gesture that says: 'Keep the neck bend'.

- Then half-halt to the outside rein in a gesture that says: 'Straighten your neck'.

- At the same time, use a little more pressure with the inside leg that says: 'Do not leave the track'.

Since the horse cannot straighten his neck because you have hold of the inside rein and he cannot swing his head and neck in front of him, he will move his shoulder in, off the track, to make his neck straight. The instant he has made a correction, back off with the rein and carry on riding him from the inside leg into the outside rein with very little inside rein.

If your horse is leg-yielding down the track – for example, he is straight through his body with no neck bend, is on four tracks, but the shoulders are the correct distance off the boards, the most likely cause is that you are asking for bend with your inside leg behind the girth. This gives quarters-out, not shoulder-in. Your inside leg must be on the girth.

Even if your horse is going well at shoulder-in and the exercise looks and feels perfectly satisfactory, be careful that you do not ask for bend with your inside leg behind the girth. This would disengage and unbalance the horse causing him to fall sideways – the opposite effect from the one intended.

To ensure that you are not committing this error, ride shoulder-in on the inside track of the school. The hind legs must remain on the inside track – it is good practice to ride shoulder-in away from the wall (off the track) – it's good for discipline and stops your horse anticipating.

One final point in respect of your leg position – at a later stage of training you will want to change shoulder-in into a half-pass and, if your have both legs back, this will create confusion.

Overall benefits of shoulder-in

Think of the shoulder-in as the basis of all lateral work and the cornerstone of all equine gymnastic exercises. If you can ride a good and correct shoulder-in, your horse should find all the other lateral movements fairly easy.

To summarize the benefits of shoulder-in:

- It is a great exercise to help straighten a horse (deal with lateral crooked-ness/one-sidedness).

- It will help supple your horse.

- It will help keep him truly and correctly on the bit.

- He will more readily accept the outside rein from the inside leg.

- It will teach him to be more aware of the directional aids from your legs. He will move away from the leg.

- It will help to balance your horse.

- It will help you to ride more accurately and to be more aware of straightness and the degree of bend and flexion in your horse.

In fact the shoulder-in is the equivalent of a human touching the toes for suppleness and press-ups for strength.

Shoulder-fore

Shoulder-fore is a lesser angle of half shoulder-in that might be used on a horse who is young or very stiff. To improve suppleness it is important that the hindquarters do not escape to the outside. The forehand must be brought to the inside. A volte can be ridden as preparation to establish flexion and bend. The forehand must be guided with both reins when the shoulder-in is gradually introduced.

However, once again – train your horse to go off your inside leg, not your inside rein. Just because you are riding shoulder-fore and not shoulder-in, don't take this as an excuse to hold on to the inside rein.

The basic aids are exactly the same as the shoulder-in, but allow the horse to keep his body straighter. It's just a question of degree and feel. Over a period of time, gradually replace the angle of shoulder-fore with the correct angle and bend of shoulder-in.

In summary

The shoulder-in is one of the easier movements to achieve if you follow the rules. I'm not saying that shoulder-in is simple – none of the lateral exercises are simple. However, it is my experience that the horse finds the concept of this movement relatively easy to understand and seems to pick up what you want very quickly. But once again I emphasize, you must follow the rules. There are two big problems you may have:

- First you will be tempted to hold on to the inside rein.

- Second, you may become tense and stiff.

Avoid both of these traits or habits, because they will really get in the way of your training.

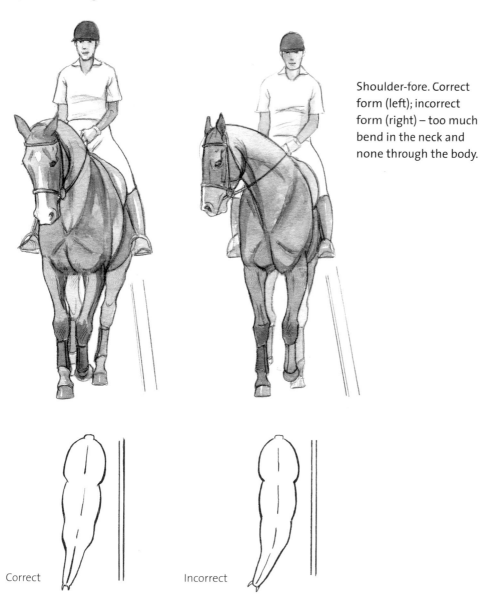

Shoulder-fore. Correct form (left); incorrect form (right) – too much bend in the neck and none through the body.

Correct   Incorrect

THE HALF-PASS

Half-pass is a lateral exercise in which the horse moves forwards and sideways, the outside legs crossing in front of the inside legs. The forehand slightly precedes the hind end, and the neck and head are flexed in the direction of the movement. Half-pass can be performed at the walk, trot, canter or even passage.

The purposes of half-pass are:

- To increase the mobility and level of attention of the horse.

- To make the horse more flexible laterally.

- To improve the range of movement of the hindquarters.

- To build up the muscles, tendons and ligaments of the limbs.

There are three rules to respect:

- The horse must go forward.

- The horse must go sideways.

- The horse must stay parallel to the wall to maintain sufficient collection during the exercise.

Although the half-pass can be ridden at a greater or lesser angle, each horse has his own correct degree of bend.

The aids

- Increase the horse's impulsion before a half-pass, maintaining cadence and rhythm.

- Position the horse's shoulders to the inside before starting.

- Keep your bending aids when leaving the wall (inside bend). The inside leg stays at the girth and controls the bend. Your seat and both legs maintain impulsion.

- The inside leg first gives the bend, then the outside leg, a little behind the girth, pushes the haunches intermittently toward half-pass.

OPPOSITE
Half-pass to the left in walk; the horse is calm and correctly positioned.

ABOVE
Half-pass right in canter.

ABOVE RIGHT
Half-pass left in trot showing crossing of the legs.

- Once the inside rein has given the bend, it then does not move anymore (although it may yield or soften.)

- The outside rein positions and controls the flexion and the horse's outside shoulder. (Therefore, it is essential that you keep a steady contact with both reins.)

- The rider's shoulders always stay parallel to the horse's shoulders. Therefore, look slightly toward the direction of the half-pass, and also turn your shoulders in the direction of the half-pass. Both seat bones take equal weight. Stretch down more with the inside leg.

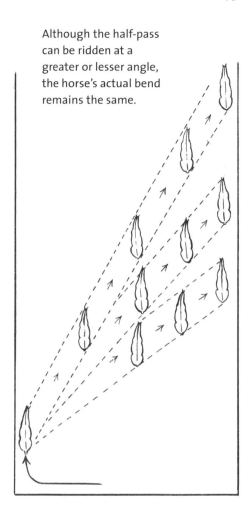

Although the half-pass can be ridden at a greater or lesser angle, the horse's actual bend remains the same.

Half-pass left in canter: an interesting moment when the diagonal pair of legs are in stance.

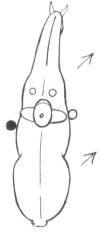

The directional aids for half-pass.

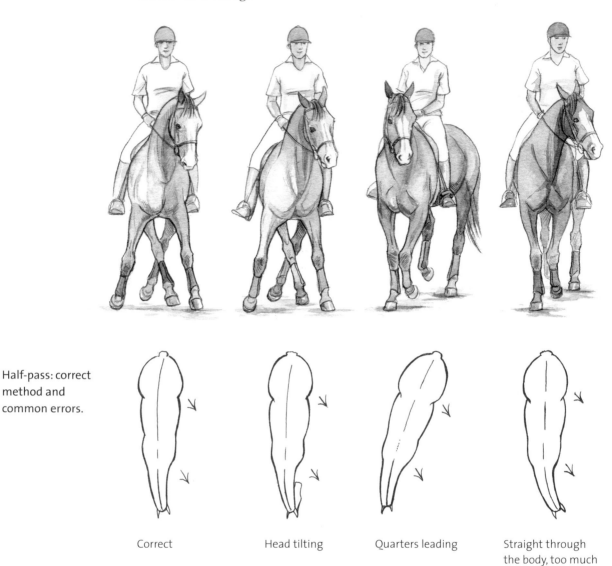

Half-pass: correct method and common errors.

Correct   Head tilting   Quarters leading   Straight through the body, too much neck bend

My advice on half-pass

- Start by riding straight along the diagonal of the school. Go forwards for a few steps before commencing the half-pass.

- Put your inside leg at the girth before leaving the wall.

- Never let the horse put more weight on one shoulder than on the other.

- Act in an intermittent manner with your inside leg – don't clamp it on.

- The outside aids must prevail (especially at the end of the half-pass), just as in a shoulder-in.

- Do not create a 'pulley effect' between your inside hand toward the withers or the other side of the neck. Move your hands in the direction of the half-pass (bringing the outside hand to the outside of the withers). This will increase the range of the half-pass stride.

- Have the same contact on both reins, never abandon the outside rein. Putting more contact on the inside rein than on the outside rein will restrain the movement.

- Make sure the horse is bent from head to tail, but do not ask for too much bend.

- Make sure you are seated well in the axis of the horse with a little more weight on the inside seat bone.

- Any adjustment made during half-pass must be done with the inside leg and the outside rein.

- To have a light inside rein, use your inside leg also. Try to replace the inside rein with the inside leg (very light rein, just for the bend).

- In a half-pass (say to the left), arrive at the wall by the corner marker, with the horse parallel, then ride straight for a stride before changing the bend for the corner, by using more inside leg and a softer left rein.

- Practise half-pass assiduously until there is no longer any resistance from the horse. Your half-pass will be good when, eventually, your horse reacts willingly to your rein and leg aids.

Teaching the young horse

- Do not teach half-pass to a horse before teaching him shoulder-in.

- Start at a walk, calmly and slowly.

- Make the horse rounded, obtain good rhythm and aim for a relaxed horse (ride a couple of steps in shoulder-in just before starting).

- After the long side of the arena, turn on to the quarter line of the short side of the arena. Take two or three strides keeping the bend (inside leg plus both reins) to position the horse's shoulders. Move your outside leg back – touch the horse in an intermittent way – and continue to touch with your inside leg well at the girth to keep the bend. Use small touches of the whip on the outside of the horse. Do not ask for too much bend. Reward after two or three lateral strides.

Ask for this two or three times on each rein, then gradually ask for a little more in the following days. Ride the half pass from a half volte in a corner to start with, and at a later stage, from a straight line. Make sure the shoulders are leading. Leg yield is also a good preparatory exercise.

My advice on teaching the young horse

- Take things very slowly at the beginning, deconstruct the movement and give the horse time to react.

- Ride a couple of shoulder-ins on the diagonal to familiarize the horse with going sideways.

- Do not hesitate to go back to shoulder-in if difficulties arise.

- Mix the half-pass work in with shoulder-in.

- Ask for less bend and more movement of the haunches when first teaching the horse, to obtain the necessary mobilization of the croup and engagement of the hind legs.

Once the horse has understood the basic concept, ask for his attention and reactivity by half-passing for three or four strides, then going straight, then asking for three or four strides of half-pass again, etc.

To half-pass from the quarter-marker to X, or on the entire diagonal, do the following in sequence.

- Start by going along the wall for two or three strides, bend the horse to the inside, position the shoulders and then ask for half-pass – so you are actually using the outside leg last.

- When turning from the wall on to the diagonal, position your inside leg at the girth before the turn to ask for more flexion and bend.

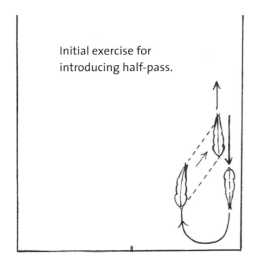

Initial exercise for introducing half-pass.

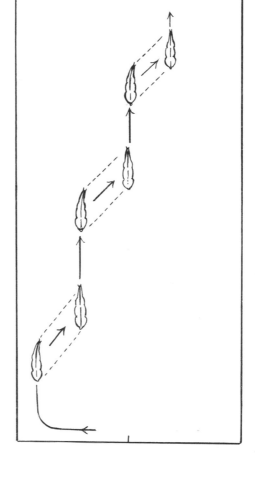

A second exercise in establishing half-pass; ride half-pass for a few strides, straighten the horse, half-pass and straighten again, repeat.

Frequently encountered problems in half-pass

How much bend should I give to a horse during half-pass?

Each horse has a degree of bend that suits him. The stronger the horse, the greater the bend will be. With young horses, the degree of bend will be less.

My horse's bend is not the same on both reins

The bend of a horse is not the same on both reins when he has one strongly concave and one strongly convex side. Minimizing such one-sidedness is part of the suppling process of training, in which astute use of the lateral exercises plays a part. As the horse becomes more supple laterally, half-pass (and much else) becomes easier.

In general, when stiffness arises, one has exceeded the degree to which the horse can curently bend correctly on that side.

My horse twists his head on the side of the half-pass

Very often, the tension of the two reins is not equal; the outside rein is forgotten, or the inside rein is too tight. Support with the outside rein and use the inside leg while softening the inside rein.

My horse quickens in half-pass

- You can slow down the movement by slightly turning your shoulders outward. Then let them come back to be parallel with the horse's shoulders.

- Use less leg.

My horse speeds up at the end of his half-pass

Stop your half-pass before the wall – that is, stop the lateral movement and send him forward 10–15 feet before the wall. Begin again and progressively half-pass all the way to the wall while reassuring the horse. You can ride the end of the half pass in walk and praise the horse.

My horse blocks his shoulders

The inside rein can sometimes (with some horses, or on one specific rein) be positioned differently. If carried away from the neck, it will spread away from the horse's shoulder and sometimes help him to half-pass without blocking the shoulders.

My horse's haunches precede the horse's shoulders

- The outside rein (and the inside rein too) must act in the direction in which the horse is going in order to put the shoulders back in place.

- The outside rein may be too far back or too strong. To correct this, soften the outside rein, half-pass four or five strides of shoulder fore, then half-pass again, straighten…

My horse's haunches are 'trailing' compared to the shoulders

Make your horse's hindquarters more active. Ride a few steps of travers, then ride straight in medium trot, collect again and travers. Repeat a few times.

My horse confuses the outside leg aid for half-pass with the aid for canter

The outside leg aid to ask for half-pass is indeed very close to the aid for the canter depart. If only the leg is used for both movements, the horse can be confused. You must therefore carefully prepare your aids and put your horse in the correct balance.

However, a canter depart should not be asked for with only the outside leg. You must also move your inside shoulder back, sit equally on both seat bones, lighten the horse's inside shoulder and move your outside leg back a little.

Also, in the canter your shoulders and the eyes are directed forward, along the axis of the horse. In the half-pass, however, you must look in the direction in which you are going, putting your shoulders parallel to the horse's shoulders.

To ask for half-pass, move your outside leg slightly further back than for the canter depart.

When first teaching the horse, do not ask for canter depart and half-pass at the same spot in the arena – rather ask for half-pass when leaving the wall on the short side of the arena, or on a diagonal, and ask for canter on a circle or on the long side of the arena.

Everything is a matter of tact, especially if your horse is 'sharp'. If you pay special attention to your preparation, your actions and your balance, your horse will learn how to differentiate the aids quickly.

This problem is also addressed from the other perspective in Frequently Encountered Problems in Canter.

TRAVERS AND RENVERS

Travers (head to the wall), renvers (croup to the wall) and half-pass are all the same family of exercises and are unrivalled for developing and confirming lateral suppleness. To produce these benefits the horse must step under properly behind and not just slide sideways. The movements should be asked for little by little, always with lightness, with the same cadence and keeping the horse 'seated'.

Introducing travers

Start at a walk, calmly and slowly. Make the horse rounded, obtain good rhythm and aim for a relaxed horse (ride shoulder-in a couple of times just before starting).

After the short side of the arena, bend the horse through the corner. Proceed on the long side, positioning the horse's forehead looking forwards along the track. Look forwards through the horse's ears. Position the horse's shoulders, keeping the bend (inside hand, inside leg). Do not ask for too much bend through the neck. Your shoulders should be parallel to the horse's shoulders. Move your outside leg back – touch the horse lightly in an intermittent way – and continue to touch with your inside leg well at the girth to keep the bend. The horse should bend around your inside leg. Use small touches of the whip on the horse's outside flank.

Give soft half-halts with the outside rein to maintain control of the outside shoulder. The outside rein allows the horse to step 'forwards, sideways'. Reward after a few lateral strides then continue straight.

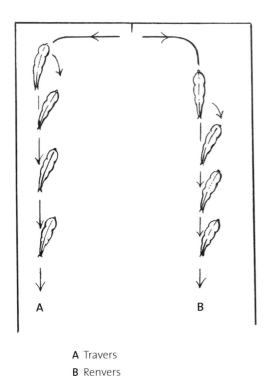

A Travers
B Renvers

Orientation and aids for renvers and travers.

Aids for riding renvers   Aids for riding travers

Inroducing renvers

Renvers is the 'mirror image' of travers: the quarters are pushed towards the wall.

Turn on to the quarter line from the short side. Proceed, positioning the horse's forehead looking forwards along the quarter line. Use the new inside rein to keep the bend.

Give soft half-halts with the outside rein to maintain control of the outside shoulder. The outside rein allows the horse to step 'forwards, sideways'.

Ask the haunches to step towards the wall. Move your outside leg back – touch the horse in an intermittent way – and continue to touch with your inside leg well at the girth to keep the bend. Use small touches of the whip on the horse's outside flank if necessary.

Renvers; the quarters towards the arena perimeter.

Travers (left half of figure) and renvers (right half of figure) can be ridden on a circle, although care must be taken to position the horse correctly, especially with travers.

The horse should bend around the rider's inside leg. Do not ask for too much bend in the neck. Reward after a few lateral strides then continue straight on the outside track.

Travers and renvers on a circle

Travers and renvers can be ridden on a circle on both reins with the haunches in and the haunches out. Many horses are inclined to crookedness by pushing the quarters to the inside so care must be taken when riding travers on a circle that the horse is correctly positioned, with flexion and bend around the rider's inside leg. Renvers on a circle (croup to the outside of the circle) is of great benefit to the suppleness of the horse.

PIROUETTES

The finished canter pirouette is a circle on two tracks, with the horse's body representing the radius of the circle: the forehand moves around the haunches, while the hind legs inscribe a circle sometimes equated to 'the size of a large dinner plate'. The horse should be prepared for pirouettes by first riding half- and full pirouettes in the walk. While these may start off as rather larger than the finished figure, the carrying power of the hindquarters is gradually increased by making the pirouettes more in place.

Quarter and half-pirouettes in canter should be ridden to improve engagement. A square is a good training exercise for introducing pirouettes, riding quarter pirouettes on each corner of the square.

Canter the square in travers with slight flexion – this should only be slight – about two hooves' width. This helps to maintain fluency in the canter. To maintain collection, quarter pirouettes should always be ridden forwards. Decreasing the size of the square is a very effective exercise for improving collection and very useful for training the half pirouette.

If the horse can take weight behind easily in the quarter pirouettes, then you can start to train the half pirouette. There are many variations for this, for example: a half- or full volte can be ridden in travers. A travers-volte is good

A canter pirouette left: the hindquarters are engaged and active; the forehand is elevated.

Canter pirouette right.

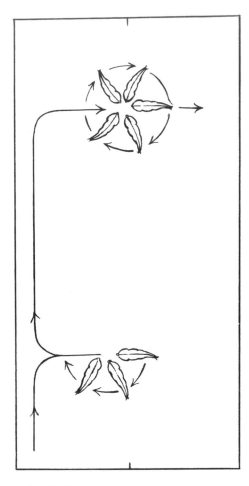

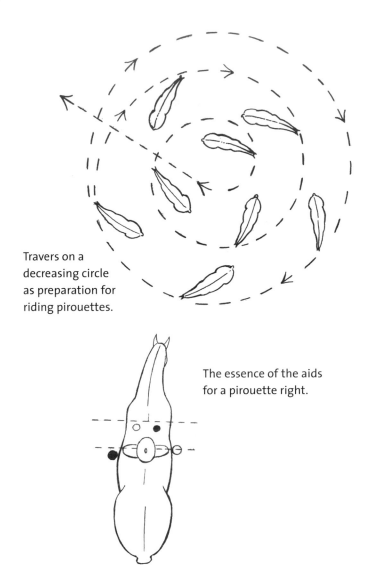

Travers on a decreasing circle as preparation for riding pirouettes.

The essence of the aids for a pirouette right.

Riding half-pirouettes (A) can be used as preparation for a full pirouette (B).

training for a full pirouette. A full pirouette should be ridden on the spot, but should you should still 'think forwards'.

Next, establish a balanced, collected canter. Bring the horse on to a circle and ride travers. Make the circle progressively smaller, maintaining the travers to make the quarters supple and then ride out of the circle with the horse straight. The canter rhythm and balance must remain, with the poll the highest point.

Once the horse can maintain collection and the canter steps are clear, then the forehand can be brought around with the rider's shoulders so that the forehand turns around the quarters in a full pirouette.

- The canter steps must be correct and in rhythm.

- If the hind feet step together then there is not enough impulsion.

- If the forehand does not remain light and raised, with the poll the highest point, then transitions between collected and medium canter should be ridden to improve the quality of the canter.

- Soft half-halts should be given with the outside rein to maintain balance and control. The inside rein asks for flexion.

- The outside leg asks behind the girth for the pirouette. The inside leg maintains impulsion and bend at the girth.

- The rider's shoulders turn with the horse.

- The rider looks between the horse's ears.

CHAPTER TEN

PIAFFE AND PASSAGE

These two highly collected, cadenced movements belong to the 'family' of trot, both having a two-beat diagonal sequence of footfall.

- In piaffe, the haunches are lowered, the hocks well engaged, the back supple and elastic, these attributes allowing great freedom, lightness and mobility of the shoulders and forehand. Although the horse shows great activity in the movement of his limbs, in the finished piaffe, he remains virtually in place – that is, he is effectively 'marking time' on the spot, with no (or absolutely minimal) forward movement.

- Passage is a highly collected, measured, elevated and cadenced trot: the legs are lifted higher than in other variants of trot and there is an accentuated period of suspension.

MY ADVICE ON PIAFFE

The piaffe is not only for the advanced horse. It is very useful for improving the carrying power of the haunches in young horses. The carrying power of the hindquarters should be evenly placed on both hind legs. Each hind foot should come off the ground as high as the fetlock on the opposite hind leg (that is, the weight-bearing one). The fetlocks should flex as the horse lowers his haunches. In a perfect piaffe, the forefeet are raised sufficiently high that the forearms are horizontal to the ground.

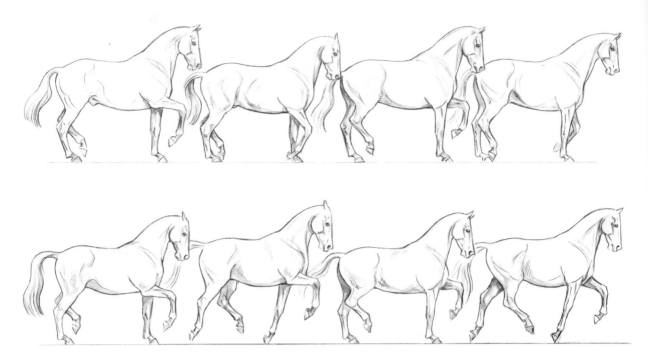

The footfalls of piaffe (above) and passage (below).

There are many ways of working in piaffe; one is by working in-hand (as mentioned in Chapter 4) where the horse can learn to flex the haunches, bend the hocks and take more weight behind without the added weight of the rider. Preparation for the ridden piaffe can either be done in-hand or under the rider by asking for higher steps in the trot.

In-hand work can be carried out either by the rider alone or with two people. The horse must first be touched with the in-hand whip lightly over the neck, over the back and on the hindquarters. The horse must understand that he is meant no harm.

My ground rules are always:

- Horse and rider must be in harmony in both body and mind, so that the horse always understands what is required of him.

- I put equal length side reins on the horse, either attached to a roller or the saddle. The side reins should bring the horse into the correct outline with the head just in front of the vertical and not behind the vertical.

- The horse must be allowed to work in a correct outline.

- The cavesson is to control the horse if strong rein aids are required. The lead rein is fastened to the centre ring on the cavesson.

ABOVE, LEFT
AND OVERLEAF ▶
Early piaffe work can
help strengthen the
horse. Correct,
progressive work
in-hand will provide
the foundation for
the ridden form.

Outlines of correct (white image) and incorrect piaffe (dark image) – see also the illustration of internal features of the movement in Chapter 4.

Transitions from walk to halt and from halt to walk are a good introduction and get the horse used to your voice. The horse must be rewarded the instant he performs what is asked of him.

The horse must always be straight.

Once the horse understands what is required, the exercise can be increased in difficulty. Transitions halt/shortened trot/halt should be used.

The hindquarters should be lightly touched with the whip. The exercises rein-back and halt improve the carrying power of the haunches.

Croup-high and on the forehand.

ABOVE AND LEFT
Errors in piaffe and passage.

Hocks out behind;
disengaged passage.

MY ADVICE ON PASSAGE

The passage can be developed from the piaffe, the trot or the walk. It very much depends on the individual horse which method is chosen: this is the choice of the rider.

The requirements for the passage are a straight horse, working correctly 'through'. The horse must be absolutely 'through' so that he can react to the lightest leg aids from the rider and forward aids from the rider's braced back without resistance.

A subtle aid from the leg, together with bracing the back and pressing the horse forwards from the lower back (loins) and a lightly restraining hand are prerequisites for the passage so that the hind legs and forelegs lift off the ground the same amount.

First, just ride a couple of steps in a row to make sure the horse is happy with the movement. It helps in the first instance to use the whip in the same moment as the aids with the lower back and legs to help the legs to lift sufficiently. Precisely how the whip is used and where it touches the quarters depends on the individual horse.

The balance between horse and rider affects the quality of the passage. In a poor passage the horse does not bring the hind legs far enough under the body. The horse who moves with stiff hips begins to swing left and right. This the wrong way, and the forelegs will cross over if the horse is not loosened up properly first.

By contrast, a good passage gives the rider the feeling of floating above the ground.

It depends on the temperament of the horse whether it offers high, springy steps, or more conservative ones. If the passage becomes shuffling, and the hind legs break out behind then the horse should be ridden in collected trot in his training. Changes of tempo will freshen and invigorate the impulsion in the movement. The activity of the hind legs will improve.

Horses who have difficulty in the passage and find it hard to keep the rhythm benefit from work in-hand. Using a cavesson and side reins give the horse a steady, even contact to work into.

If doing this, the piaffe should be used first to get rid of any stiffness and to improve engagement. After a few steps of passage, the horse should be allowed to go forwards into trot. As soon as the horse has offered some good steps of passage, he should be rewarded.

OPPOSITE
Two views of passage.

IN CONCLUSION

To conclude this book, I would like to revisit some key points I made in my introduction. Chief among these is that classical training aims to enhance every aspect of a horse's existence. Not only is the classically trained horse fit, strong, supple and obedient; he also enjoys longevity and the calm and happy existence that comes from truly understanding what is required of him.

In order for this to occur, he must be trained by a rider who truly understands how horses think and learn, and who – in addition to building mental rapport with the horse – has the technical ability to sit consistently in balance with him and to apply the aids in harmonious combinations, that the horse can interpret and comply with readily.

These technical attributes in the rider can only be attained by much thought, study and practice. Ignoring faults in the seat and trying to achieve rapid progress by rough and inappropriate methods will never produce results which are truly satisfactory – let alone classical.

We have to admit that riding is an endeavour in which there is no absolute pinnacle of success, because no horse and no human is perfect. However, the fact that perfection is elusive does not mean that we should not strive towards it, seeking always to improve our technical skill and our understanding of the horse. This, indeed, is the most assured way of achieving those moments of complete harmony with our horses which, although often transitory, give us the basis for building a true partnership, from which we and our horses will assuredly benefit.

In his book, *Principles of Dressage*, Kurt Albrecht, a former Director of the Spanish Riding School, wrote:

> Most of the cases of resistance or even open rebellion by the horse are founded upon that most human of all human attributes, which is to forgive one's own weaknesses and to be intolerant of the weakness of others.

Taking this observation to heart, let us riders be ever-vigilant and demanding of the highest standards in ourselves, and ever-ready to allow our horses the time, patience and respect they deserve.

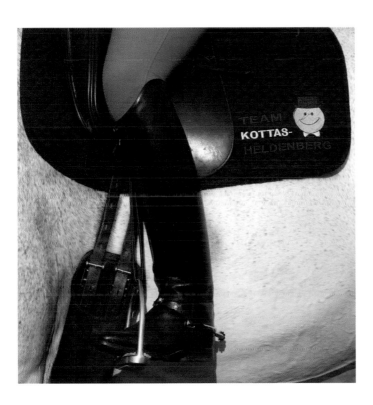

GLOSSARY

Cadence Derived from the Latin *cado* = fall, cadence is a musical term borrowed by equitation to signify a clear, regular and correct sequence of footfall.

Cavalletti Literally, 'little horses' in Italian. Wooden rails fastened asymmetrically at both ends to small cross- or block-shaped supports, so that their height can be adjusted. Used in a series (three or more) to help regulate stride length and to work the horse's limbs and back; can be employed as a training aid either under saddle or on the lunge. It is important that spacing and height are appropriate for the horse's level of training and the gait being worked upon.

Collection Describes a state in which the horse, having developed strength in the hindquarters through correct, progressive training, uses the strength in this area to carry a greater proportion of his and the rider's weight, thus improving his balance and poise. The altered balance and lowered hindquarters increase the ratio of lift to thrust in the hindquarters, producing characteristically elevated, animated steps. There is a lightening of the forehand, with the poll the highest point, and the horse flexes readily at poll and jaw. While a relatively untrained, unfit horse can adopt a collected pose momentarily, as a reaction to excitement or danger, he cannot maintain this posture for any length of time because he lacks the muscular development necessary. For the same reason, attempts to force a partly trained horse into a 'collected' outline are counterproductive and may actually cause damage. The development of true collection is a long-term process.

Descente de jambes A term from French equitation; a reduction of the rider's leg aids, especially to reward or acknowledge the horse's willingness to move forwards.

Descente de main A term from French equitation; basically, a yielding of the rein contact, either as reward or to check the horse's self-balance. In respect of the hands, 'descente' can mean either a physical lowering, or a 'reduction' (lessening) of the contact – commonly, both.

Descente de main et de jambes A simultaneous reduction in the demands of the rider's legs and hands (see above).

Engagement The hind limbs are said to be engaged when, during the forward (stance) phase of movement, they are placed sufficiently forward under the horse's mass to enhance balance and provide a good level of propulsion/lift.

Extension The lengthening of an individual horse's stride to its practical maximum, without compromising the balance or regularity of footfall. The degree of extension achievable will be governed by a horse's conformation, but will be assisted by the gradual development of joint flexibility, muscular strength, balance and impulsion.

Free walk A form of walk in which the horse is given freedom to stretch his head and neck on a long rein; the walk should remain regular and active with big steps that clearly overtrack by two horseshoe's length.

Flying change At canter, the change of leading leg from left to right, or vice versa, accomplished within a single stride with no intervening trot or walk strides. A good flying change is 'clean' (the sequence of legs is changed correctly and precisely), balanced and straight.

Gait variant A specific form of an individual gait. The forms specified by the rules of competition dressage are (for walk) free, collected, medium, extended and for trot and canter collected, working, medium and extended. Particularly heightened forms of the collected gaits have traditionally been known as 'school gaits'.

Half-pass A lateral movement performed across diagonals of the arena. The horse is bent slightly round the inside leg of the rider, and looks in the direction of the movement; his outside legs pass and cross in front of his inside legs.

N.B. In canter half-pass, the legs do not cross; rather the horse 'bounds' forwards and sideways, maintaining balance and inside bend.

There is a general requirement that, regardless of the angle at which half-pass is performed, the horse's body should remain approximately parallel to the side of the arena; this 'approximate' requirement relating to the fact that there is an element of bend in the horse's body and that the forehand should be slightly 'leading' the hindquarters (thus the slightly 'bent' horse cannot be truly parallel to a straight line). The half-pass can be performed at various angles but the greater the angle (i.e. the more 'sideways' movement required) the harder it is for the horse to maintain the desired characteristics of the movement.

Impulsion The propulsive energy generated by the horse's hindquarters and controlled by the rider's leg, seat and reins.

In-hand Exercising or schooling a horse whilst dismounted, at close quarters, commonly using a short line to connect trainer to horse, or working the horse directly from the bridle.

Inside The side of the horse currently showing some degree of lateral concavity.

Lateral movements Those which require some element of 'sideways' movement in addition to forward movement: they include turn on the forehand, leg-yielding, shoulder-in, half-pass, travers, renvers and pirouettes. The most highly regarded of these movements, in terms of the benefits it brings to the horse's development, is shoulder-in but, performed correctly, all make some contribution towards educating and suppling the horse.

Leg-yielding A lateral movement in which the horse moves forwards and to some degree sideways in response to pressure from the rider's inside leg. The horse's body remains nearly straight, with just a slight flexion at the poll; the inside legs pass and cross in front of the outside legs. This is generally used as a fairly early training exercise, to teach response to the rider's leg and to improve suppleness of the limbs.

Lengthening Basically, an increase in the length of strides from those currently being performed. However, the term is commonly used to signify a relatively modest increase in stride length from the working gait. Thus, while 'medium' and 'extended' gaits are specific forms of lengthening, 'lengthening' will often be used to describe a young horse whose strides are longer than the working gait but perhaps short of a fully formed medium gait with its associated qualities of increased levels of engagement, balance and cadence.

Medium A term used to describe what might otherwise be termed the horse's 'everyday' walk, where the hind feet touch the ground beyond the front hoof-prints ('overtrack'). However, in respect of trot and canter, it describes a somewhat lengthened form of gait between 'working' and 'extended'. In these two gaits, there is not only an increase in the use of the limbs, but also more movement/ rounding of the back and increased engagement of the hindquarters.

One-time changes A series of flying changes of canter lead, performed every stride.

Outside The side of the horse currently showing some degree of convexity.

Passage A powerful, highly collected and elevated development of the trot, with prolonged periods of suspension.

Piaffe A form of movement that was, historically (and still is, in some classical schools) used to prepare the horse for the 'airs above the ground' but is nowadays seen more widely as evidence of advanced levels of collection. Piaffe is a highly elevated diagonal movement of the limbs in two-time, more or less on the spot, with lowered quarters, the forelimbs thus showing greater elevation than the hind limbs. Although (as with collection generally) work *towards* piaffe can begin at a relatively early stage of a horse's education, the finished form of the movement requires considerable strength in the horse and thus should not be contemplated at too early a stage.

Pirouette A movement in which the horse turns through 360 degrees, on a very small circle, by pivoting around the inside hind leg. This leg 'marks time' by being raised and lowered almost on the spot in the rhythm of the gait, while the outside hind describes a very small circle around it; the forehand describing a second circle with a circumference in the order of 7 metres, the radius of this circle being roughly equivalent to the length of the horse. The whole figure is executed in 6–8 strides. Pirouettes can be performed in collected walk, collected canter and piaffe; the finished forms require gradual development, for instance via demi-pirouettes (half-pirouettes through 180 degrees)

Rein-back The form of backward progression in the horse. The horse moves at pretty much the same tempo as in walk, but the steps are taken in diagonal pairs (as in trot). The movement should be straight, regular, unhurried and uncon-strained. Correct rein-back cannot be achieved by the rider 'pulling' the horse backwards; it must result from a redirection of the basic 'forward' impulse.

Renvers Also known as croup to the wall, or haunches out, renvers is a lateral movement that is the mirror image of travers. In renvers, the hindquarters remain on the prescribed track while the forehand is displaced to the inside; the horse looks in the direction of movement.

Rhythm Essentially, a repeated pattern of sound. Note that *repetition* is the key point in defining rhythm, thus a horse may exhibit a *regular* rhythm without that rhythm being *correct*. As an extreme example, a lame horse might exhibit a repeated 1,2,3, hop rhythm at walk, instead of the correct, regular 1,2,3,4. Furthermore, since an individual horse will have a rhythm that is appropriate for him at each gait, there exists the possibility that he may sometimes deviate from this and display a rhythm that is too fast, or too slow.

'School' gaits A term rooted in the *haute école* (high school) academic and artistic equitation of earlier centuries. This equitation placed great emphasis on the development of a refined form of collection and the 'school' gaits represented the pinnacle of collection.

Shortening Basically, a decrease in the length of strides from those currently being performed. However, the term 'shortened' was traditionally used to signify a relatively modest decrease in stride length (with no decrease in energy) from the working gaits. Working young horses (particularly) in slightly shortened trot and canter is one of the early steps along the road towards developing collection.

Shoulder-in A lateral movement in which the horse, bent throughout his body, moves at an angle of about 30 degrees to the direction of travel, with his head flexed away from the direction of movement. His inside hind leg steps forward and under his body, in advance of but not across his outside hind; his inside foreleg passes in front of the outer, requiring some extra lift of the knee. The chief benefits of the movement are that it enhances engagement (especially of the inside hind), thereby having a collecting effect, frees the shoulders and lightens the forehand and supples the hindquarters and the whole of the body laterally. While the 'normal' form of shoulder-in (that required in competition) is the 30 degree version performed on three tracks (1. outside hind, 2. inside hind and outside fore, 3. inside fore), supple and highly schooled horses may be able to perform a four-line version, at a greater angle but, in this latter form, it is essential that the lateral bend is maintained, otherwise the gymnastic benefits will be lost.

Tempi changes A sequence of flying changes performed after a prescribed number of strides, e.g. every fourth stride. 'One-time' changes require a flying change every stride.

Transitions within gaits Changes between one form of a particular gait and another, e.g. collected to extended trot.

Travers Also known as head to the wall or haunches in, travers is a lateral movement that may be performed along the outside track or, indeed, in relation to any other prescribed track, with the horse looking in the direction of the movement. While it is required in some dressage tests, its primary schooling value is as a suppling exercise of the lateral muscles and hind limbs.

Turn on the Forehand A turn in which the horse pivots around his inside foreleg, which marks the (walk) time of the movement. An early exercise in lateral movement, it is useful in that respect, but should not be overdone, since it lacks real forward movement and can tend to move the horse's centre of gravity forward (i.e. towards the forehand).

INDEX

(numbers in italics refer to illustrations)